Zion's Joy
by Jeremiah Burroughs
with chapters by C. Matthew McMahon

Copyright Information

Zion's Joy, by Jeremiah Burroughs with chapters by C. Matthew McMahon
Edited by Therese B. McMahon

Changes made to this edition do not affect the overall language of the document, nor do they change the writer's intention. Spelling, grammar, and formatting changes have been made, and modernized wording is used in specific cases to help today's reader more fully grasp the intention of the author.

Copyright © 2012, 2025 2nd Edition by Puritan Publications and A Puritan's Mind

Published by Puritan Publications
A Ministry of A Puritan's Mind
Crossville, TN
www.puritanpublications.com
www.apuritansmind.com
www.gracechapeltn.com
www.reformedsynod.com

All rights reserved. No part of this publication may be reproduced, stored in a retrieval system or transmitted in any form by any means, electronic, mechanical, photocopy, recording or otherwise, without the prior permission of the publisher, except as provided by USA copyright law.

First Edition, 2012
Second Edition, 2025
Manufactured in the United States of America

eISBN: 978-1-937466-60-2
ISBN: 978-1-937466-61-9

Table of Contents

Meet Jeremiah Burroughs 4

God's Work of Reformation 13

Preface 22

Part 1: Zion's Joy 26

Part 2: Rejoice with Jerusalem 30

Part 3: Doctrine 37

Part 4: The Third Doctrine 51

Part 5: Reasons of Jerusalem's Joy 58

Part 6: A Call to Rejoice: 71

Other Works at Puritan Publications by Burroughs
.... 103

Meet Jeremiah Burroughs
By C. Matthew McMahon, Ph.D., Th.D.

Jeremiah Burroughs (1599–1646) was a man set apart by his unwavering commitment to the Gospel and a tender but resolute passion for peace within the church. Born into an age of ecclesiastical turbulence, his life was a vivid testimony to the cost of Christian conviction and the extraordinary mercy of God. His ministry, shaped by both persecution and restoration, serves as a clarion call to those who value reformation, not merely as a theological principle but as a way of life grounded in holiness, humility, and the love of truth.

Educated at Cambridge University, Burroughs was not just a scholar but a minister marked by pastoral wisdom and a tireless dedication to his calling. Yet his nonconformity to the Church of England's rites, particularly under the tightening grip of episcopal rule, led to his suspension from ministry and his eventual exile. Burroughs' story is one of perseverance amid hardship and a deep, abiding trust in the sovereignty of God—a theme he would later weave into the rich depth of his sermons and writings.

A Ministry Tested by Fire

After completing his studies, Burroughs was appointed as a colleague to Edmund Calamy at Bury St. Edmund's. In 1631, he was called to serve as minister at Tivetshall in Norfolk. However, his tenure was cut short when Bishop Wren issued his notorious *Visitation Articles* in 1633, aimed at enforcing strict ecclesiastical conformity. Burroughs, unable to compromise his conscience, was deprived of his livelihood and forced to leave his flock.

During this time, he sought refuge under the protection of the patriotic Earl of Warwick, who admired Burroughs' integrity. However, even the Earl's influence could not shield him indefinitely. The storm of persecution grew too fierce, and Burroughs fled to Holland, where he settled in Rotterdam and joined the esteemed Rev. William Bridge as a teacher in the congregational church. It was here, amidst a congregation of exiles, that Burroughs continued his work as a preacher of "peaceable reformation."

Yet, Burroughs' exile was marred by controversy. Critics like Mr. Edwards accused him of seditious intent, claiming that Burroughs fled out of fear after opposing the war with Scotland. In response, Burroughs defended himself with characteristic grace, stating that he had spoken with discretion and had nothing to fear but the biased power of those who sought his ruin. His accuser, he explained, had distorted the truth, ignoring the months that passed before he departed and the invitation from the church in Rotterdam that called him to minister abroad.

A Return to England: Preacher of Peace

When the English Civil War shifted the balance of power, Burroughs returned to England. His aim was not to sow sedition but to preach peace. His sermons were marked by a genuine pastoral care for the *unity* of Christ's church. Preaching in Stepney at seven in the morning and at Cripplegate later in the day, Burroughs ministered to some of the largest congregations in England, earning the admiration of many. Alongside William Greenhill, he was known as one of the "morning and evening stars" of Stepney.

Burroughs' influence extended beyond the pulpit to the Westminster Assembly, where he was chosen as one of the divines tasked with establishing a unified doctrine for the reformed church. Despite his alignment with the independent, or congregational, view of church governance—believing each congregation should govern itself without external coercion—Burroughs was revered for his humility and moderation. Unlike many in the heat of debate, he sought unity without compromising truth, embodying the spirit of his Savior in every dispute.

The Call for Liberty of Conscience

Burroughs' role in the Westminster Assembly (1643–1653) highlights his commitment to sound doctrine and the peace of the church amidst one of the most significant theological gatherings in history. Chosen as one of the independent divines, Burroughs participated in the assembly tasked with reforming the doctrine, worship, and governance of the Church of England. His contributions, though shaped by his belief in congregational independence rather than presbyterial governance, were marked by a spirit of humility and a desire for unity rooted in biblical truth. Burroughs stood alongside other notable figures like Thomas Goodwin and Philip Nye, articulating the conviction that church authority must rest solely upon the Scriptures and that each congregation, under Christ's headship, must be free from external spiritual coercion.

Burroughs' unwavering commitment to liberty of conscience became a hallmark of his ministry. He joined Thomas Goodwin, Philip Nye, and others in publishing the *Apologetical Narration*, defending the principle that each congregation was to be governed according to Scripture, free from the coercive power of centralized authority. Burroughs and his fellow independents held that the sword should never be used to force religious conformity. In one of his most poignant declarations, he asserted that the attempt to enforce uniformity through fines, imprisonment, and persecution only fostered discord and suppressed truth.

His words remain timeless: "So long as men think there can be no religious peace without forcing all into one opinion... the Christian world shall remain a scene of animosity and universal discord." Burroughs foresaw that the refusal to honor Christian liberty would lead to strife rather than true unity.

The Ministry of Healing: *Irenicum* and Final Years

Burroughs' final years were marked by a grief over the divisions within the church and a desire to heal them. His last work, *Irenicum, or An Attempt to Heal the Divisions among Christian Professors*, was a heartfelt appeal for peace. In it, he lamented the pride and contention that had fractured the body of Christ and called believers back to humility and mutual forbearance.

The strain of constant preaching and the weight of the church's divisions took a toll on Burroughs' health. In 1646, at the age of forty-seven, he succumbed to consumption. Though his life was brief, his legacy endured. As Mr. Granger wrote, "He was a man of learning, candor, and modesty; in his life irreproachable, and highly exemplary." His writings, beloved by many, continue to edify the church today.

A Legacy of Faithful Teaching

Burroughs' works reflect the heart of a shepherd who longed for his flock to understand the depth of God's mercy. His expository sermons, particularly his celebrated *Exposition of Hosea*, showcased his skill in applying Scripture to the varied trials of his hearers. Among his most well-known works is *The Rare Jewel of Christian Contentment*, a treatise that teaches believers to rest in God's providence, even in adversity. His *Gospel Worship* reminds readers of the reverence due to God in worship, echoing the biblical call to approach Him with awe and gratitude.

One of Burroughs' central convictions was the necessity of being "underneath the blood" of Christ. He believed that true reformation began not with external conformity but with the cleansing and covering of Christ's blood. This foundational truth animated all of his writings and preaching.

Conclusion

Jeremiah Burroughs stands as a light of faithful

reformation—a man who pursued unity without forsaking doctrine, who preached peace without tolerating error, and who endured hardship with unwavering trust in God's promises. His commitment to Christ and His church challenges modern readers to consider the cost of true faithfulness.

In our age, where disagreements over worship and governance often divide the church, Burroughs' life and teachings remind us that true reformation flows from hearts washed in the blood of the Lamb and united in humble *obedience to His Word*. As he himself taught, the Christian's joy is not found in earthly security or human approval but in the unshakable truth that Christ has shed His blood for His people. In this, believers are called to rejoice, for they are eternally secured in His grace.

His Works are divided into two sections here, modernized, and those still in old English.

Modernized Works (which can be found at *Puritan Publications*):

1. Jerusalem's Glory Breaking Forth into the World.
2. Spots of the Godly and of the Wicked.
3. The Saint's Inheritance and the Worldling's Portion.

4. Zion's Joy.[1]
5. Gospel Peace.
6. Jacob's Seed and David's Delight.
7. Christ Inviting Sinners to Himself.
8. Gospel Worship.
9. Rules for Our Walking with God.
10. The Excellency of Holy Courage in Evil Times.
11. The Glorious Name of God the Lord of Hosts.
12. The Excellency of Jesus Christ.
13. The Excellent Name of God.
14. The Wonders of Jesus.
15. The Excellency of the Soul

Works still in Old English:

1. Moses' Choice.
2. An Exposition of the Prophecy of Hosea.
3. The Lord's Heart Opened.
4. A Vindication of Mr. Burroughs against Mr. Edward's Foul Aspersions, in his spreading Gangarena, and his angry Antapologia, concerning Independency.
5. Irenicum, to the Lovers of Truth and Peace.
6. Two Treatises, the first of Earthlimindedness,

---

[1] September 7, 1641. Based on Psalm 147:2, The Lord doth build up Jerusalem: he gathereth together the outcasts of Israel. Published by the order of the said House. (London, Printed by T.P. and M.S. for R. Dawlman, and Are to be sold by Ben Alline in Popes Head Alley, 1641).

the second of Conversing in Heaven.
7. The Rare Jewell of Christian Contentment.
8. Gospel Conversation.
9. The Evil of Evils, or the Exceeding Sinfulness of Sin.
10. The Saint's Treasury.
11. Of Hope and Faith, and the Saint's Walk by Faith.
12. Reconciliation, or Christ's Trumpet of Peace.
13. The Saint's Happiness.
14. True Blessedness, which consists in the pardon of sin.

God's Work of Reformation
by C. Matthew McMahon, Ph.D., Th.D.

Isaiah 66:10, "Rejoice ye with Jerusalem, and be glad with her, all ye that love her: rejoice for joy with her, all ye that mourn for her."

If there's one thing that can shake a man to his core, it's witnessing the mighty hand of God work unexpectedly and irresistibly, like an unseen current that sweeps you clean off your feet and sets you down where you least expected to be. Jeremiah Burroughs, in his masterful appeal to the church, takes this truth by the collar and holds it up for all to see. His words tumble out in depth of reverence, warning, and hope—each thread colored by Scripture and steeped in the conviction that when God begins His work of reformation, no man can stop it, no matter how fierce the opposition or how tangled the circumstances.

Burroughs stood as a man wholly convinced that the glory of God in His church was the noblest cause a Christian could labor for. He wasn't merely trying to adjust a crooked painting or trim a few unkempt branches—he was pointing to the root. And his message is simple at its core: when God brings about reformation, His people must not sit idly by. They must rise with praise in their hearts, strength in their souls, and reverence in their steps, knowing that the Master Builder does not abandon His work halfway through.

The Call to Rejoice in God's Mercy

Burroughs' foundation rests squarely on Isaiah 66:10, "Rejoice ye with Jerusalem, and be glad with her, all ye that love her: rejoice for joy with her, all ye that mourn for her." It's not merely a suggestion; it's a call to arms for the sincere heart. *Rejoice* because God has not left His people to wallow in despair. Rejoice because the covenantal mercies of God—sealed by the blood of Christ—are not fragile threads that can snap with the whims of earthly powers. When the saints cry out in their troubles, God hears. And when He answers with mercy, there's no room for faint applause or half-hearted murmurs of thanks.

Burroughs knew firsthand that the Christian life is no placid stroll through green meadows. It's a battle, a pilgrimage through thorns and deserts. But he also knew that the darkest trials are often the stage upon which God's brightest mercies appear. He points to the saints of old who suffered reproach for clinging to God's promises—those men and women who, when despised by the world, clung *tighter* to Christ. And he insists that when deliverance comes, it must be met not with quiet relief but with resounding joy.

In his exposition of Isaiah's words, Burroughs paints a picture of the church that is *both* aching and triumphant. He reminds his readers of the imagery of Israel's exodus—of blood-marked doorposts and the passing over of death. God's people knew fear, but they also knew the joy of protection and salvation. In much the same way, the Christian stands under the blood of Christ, spared from wrath and called to rejoice.

The Mercy of Deliverance Without Travail

One of Burroughs' keen observations lies in the surprising nature of God's mercy. Drawing from Isaiah 66:7, "Before she travailed, she brought forth; before her pain came, she was delivered of a man child," he reflects on how God often spares His people from the full weight of suffering they expect. England, in Burroughs' time, had narrowly escaped the bloody fate of other nations embroiled in religious wars. The land could have been soaked with the blood of its people, but instead, God intervened, bringing forth reformation and peace with a surprising swiftness.

To Burroughs, this was *no* mere coincidence—it was the deliberate hand of God bringing mercy where ruin had seemed certain. And he warns against the thanklessness that sometimes arises when deliverance comes too easily. Just because the labor pains were brief doesn't make the birth any less miraculous. He presses his readers to see the sheer magnitude of God's kindness and to understand that it deserves more than a passing nod—it demands exuberant gratitude and unwavering trust.

The Triumph Over Reproach and Shame

Burroughs was acutely aware of the scorn the saints faced *in the pursuit of holiness.* He recalls the mockery hurled at the Puritans, called "precise" and "scrupulous" for holding to *God's commands* while others bent with the winds of worldly approval. But he assures his readers that such reproach will not endure. Citing Isaiah 66:5, "Your brethren that hated you, that cast you out for my name's sake, said, Let the Lord be glorified: but he shall appear to your joy, and they shall be ashamed"—he reminds the faithful that their vindication will come.

The world has always had its Sanballats and Tobiahs—men who sneer at the work of God and seek to hinder it with ridicule and cunning. But Burroughs insists that the schemes of such men will collapse under the weight of God's justice. The enemies of Jerusalem may howl and gnash their teeth, but in the end, they will be the ones put to shame, while the faithful stand secure in their joy.

The Blood That Covers All

For Burroughs, all of this—the joy, the mercy, the victory—flows *directly* from *the cross of Christ*. The reformation of the church isn't just a matter of polity or ceremony; *it's a matter of living under the cleansing, shielding blood of the Lamb*. He emphasizes that the Christian's only hope in life and death is to be found "underneath the blood," shielded from the wrath of God by the sacrifice of Christ.

Burroughs returns time and again to this central truth: without the shedding of blood, there is no remission of sins (Hebrews 9:22). The Old Testament sacrifices were but shadows of the true sacrifice to come. Christ's blood was not spilled haphazardly—it was poured out as the fulfillment of every covenant promise. And when a believer stands underneath that blood, he stands as one acquitted, redeemed, and restored.

A Charge to Persevere

As Burroughs moves toward his conclusion, he turns his focus to the responsibilities that come with such remarkable mercy. To be saved by grace doesn't mean to sit idle or to bask in complacency. It means living in obedience and pressing forward in the work of the Lord with renewed strength. He calls the church to be steadfast, even when weariness sets in.

Drawing from Nehemiah's resolve in rebuilding Jerusalem's walls, Burroughs warns against giving in to fear or faltering in the face of opposition. God's work of reformation requires constancy—what began with prayer and courage must be crowned with perseverance. And those who hold fast to the end will find that their labor was not in vain, for the beauty of the Lord will rest upon them, establishing the work of their hands.

Jeremiah Burroughs' message is as timely now as it was when he first wrote it. The call to rejoice with Jerusalem is more than an invitation to celebration—it's a command to trust in God's sovereign hand and to live in the assurance that what He has begun, He will surely bring to completion. Burroughs understood that reformation isn't merely about outward change but about the heart's response to the mercy of God.

The Christian who finds himself under the blood of Christ has every reason to rejoice, *no matter* the trials that come his way. For the same God who brought forth mercy before the pains of travail will not abandon His work midway. The church must rise in gratitude and courage, knowing that the victory belongs to the Lord. And as long as the saints lift their eyes heavenward and stand upon His promises, they will find themselves, like Jerusalem of old, a city not forsaken but crowned with joy and gladness.

Final Side Note on Jeremiah Burroughs and the Westminster Assembly: Reformation, Resistance, and the Antichrist's Undoing

If ever there was a time when a man of God had to balance a heart full of peace with a mind sharp as iron, it was the *Westminster Assembly*, and Jeremiah Burroughs was just the sort to walk that line (he's one of my favorite preachers). He was no firebrand preacher foaming at the mouth with reckless zeal, nor was he the type to sit quiet while error crept through the doors of the church like a thief in the night. He stood between two extremes—unyielding in truth yet pleading for unity, a reformer with a heart as large as his doctrine was sound.

At the Westminster Assembly (1643–1653), where England's greatest theological minds gathered to hammer out the church's doctrine, Burroughs held fast to his Independent convictions. He saw clearly what was at stake. The Church of England had been bruised by prelatical tyranny, and now the Presbyterians sought to reform it—but their method, he feared, still left room for the same old chains under a new name. To him, true reformation wasn't merely reshuffling who sat in power, but rather ensuring that no man—bishop, presbyter, or king—would set himself up as lord over another's conscience.

This was no mere squabble over church polity. It was a battle for the purity of Christ's church and a stand against the rising smoke of *Antichrist*—the Roman Catholic church itself—that had *darkened* Christendom for centuries. Burroughs knew the papacy was not some minor corruption in the church, some slight error that could be patched up with councils and clever compromises. No, it was the great enemy of Christ, the seat of idolatry, and the counterfeit kingdom that had dared to place itself in God's temple, as Paul warned in 2 Thessalonians 2:3–4. Isaiah 66:10–11 was a banner for his cause—"Rejoice ye with Jerusalem, and be glad with her, all ye that love her." For Burroughs, this was no idle call to optimism but a rallying cry for faithful souls who longed for a church free from the yoke of Antichrist. Jerusalem—the true church—was suffering under oppression, but God had not forsaken her. There was a child to be born, a great work of reformation, and though there would be labor pains, it would come to pass.

Burroughs fought against Rome, not with carnal weapons, but with the sword of *truth and purity*. He warned his brethren: *If you leave room for power-hungry men to rule the church, Rome will rise again, dressed in a new garb, but the same beast underneath.* The Reformation had shaken the great harlot, but she was ever lurking, seeking to draw men back into her nets.

His plea to the Assembly was simple: reform, but do not replace one tyranny with another. Let Christ govern His own church through His Word, and let no man lay burdens where God has not. The Antichrist's power was already judged by heaven, but it was the duty of faithful men to *stand firm, proclaim truth, and see the work through*. For Christ would not bring forth this child of reformation only to let it be stillborn. God had begun a great work, and He would finish it.

In Christ's grace and mercy,
C. Matthew McMahon, Ph.D., Th.D.
From My study, February, 2025
"...search the Scriptures..." (John 5:39).
www.apuritansmind.com
www.puritanpublications.com
www.gracechapeltn.com
www.reformedsynod.com

Preface

To the Honorable Knights, Citizens, and Burgesses of the House of Commons in Parliament,

If it is the greatest happiness for a person on earth to serve as an instrument for God, then God has truly made you most blessed. Complete the work you have begun among us, and blessed be the time that you were born and have lived to see this day. The generations yet to be born will rise up and bless you. Consider the promise the Father made to Christ in Isaiah 49:8: "In an acceptable time have I heard thee." This promise is now fulfilled for His church. Indeed, it was a most acceptable time when God heard the prayers of His people by assembling this Honorable Body so providentially and sustaining you to be a continual blessing to all His servants, as you have indeed been. You came together through prayer, you stand by prayer, and your success here is a blessed fruit of prayer. The prayers of countless thousands of saints rest upon *you* daily.

Continue, most noble and worthy senators; press on and prosper. The Lord is with you. We all bow in humble petition, beseeching you to finish what you have so admirably begun. You are engaged in as honorable a service for God and His people as any assembly has ever been since the world began. You have been given a sacred opportunity to exalt the name of the great God, to cause godliness to be respected in the world, and to remove the contempt and scorn that have been cast upon it. Do this to defend the liberties of your nation so that men may live as men and as Christians, in all godliness and honesty, with peace. In so doing, you will make your own names *renowned* for generations to come.

Let your own personal desires, opinions, and ambitions be set aside and wholly absorbed in the great public work to which you are called. This great trust has been committed to you, and you are *accountable* for it. Let your actions be like the heavens—moved swiftly by the hand of God, but deliberate in your own movements. Christ said, "And I, if I be lifted up from the earth, will draw all men unto me" (John 12:32). In the same way, if you exalt godliness, all people will come to honor it. Even if you were to live no longer beyond this act of service, this alone would be worth your lives. Indeed, your lives—precious to us as they are—would still be worth this cost, even if they were many thousands of times more valuable.

Those who love Jerusalem will rejoice with her—how much more, then, will those who, out of love for her, bring her joy? Those who once mourned for her will be glad. May the blessing of those hearts that you have comforted rest upon you and your descendants after you. You, who have been so instrumental for the good of Zion, may the Lord, the Maker of heaven and earth, bless you from Zion. After so many days of mourning in and for England, God has, through you, given us a day of rejoicing—a pledge, we hope, of many more joyful days to come.

    For my part, not long ago I would have considered it a blessing simply to live peacefully in my country and be useful to my brethren, even if it meant mourning with them all my days. But now I am called to rejoice, and though I could have done so from the solitude of my chamber, it would have been a service I was unworthy of. To be called to rejoice and praise God publicly, before and alongside this great congregation of our Honorable Leaders—to help you rejoice and praise God, to be your voice in blessing God, and to be God's voice to you in stirring your hearts to bless Him—this is truly a service. I can say no more of it than this: it is as far beyond what I had ever imagined as it is beyond my capacity, and that is a vast distance indeed.

    Now that you have called me to another service, to publish what I have previously delivered, I have complied, though it was a task not without difficulty. Yet it is not as daunting as the first. The former task was the sanctifying of God's name in one of the greatest services ever offered to Him by England (as I teach in "Gospel Worship"—that "God will be sanctified by those who draw near to Him"[2]). In that moment, I feared lest God's name should suffer because of my own

---

[2] Republished and modernized by Puritan Publications.

weakness. But this task is different—it is an act of obedience to your request. I present to you not only the content of what I delivered but all that I could recover from my notes. Certain points were omitted previously due to limited time, or because certain expressions came to me spontaneously as I transcribed my notes. I did not intend or attempt to make any additions.

May the Lord bless you abundantly and gloriously in the great matters entrusted to you. While you labor, we shall be praying and praising. I consider it a blessing that I may live to join those who do so—who remain,

Your Honors' devoted servant in all Christian duty,
JEREMIAH BURROUGHS

Part 1:
Zion's Joy

Isaiah 66:10, "Rejoice ye with Jerusalem, and be glad with her, all ye that love her: rejoice for joy with her, all ye that mourn for her."

Today, we have a cause for great rejoicing in the same spirit of this scripture. In Leviticus 3:6, we read of the acceptable peace offering to the Lord, which could be a female from the flock: "If his offering for a sacrifice of peace offering unto the LORD be of the flock, male or female, he shall offer it without blemish." In this spirit, today we offer God a peace offering, for this is indeed a day of thanksgiving. Although I may have but a humble "female" to bring to this sacred service of the Lord—a reference to the simplicity and humility of my offering—I cannot withdraw from the work to which both God and this *Honorable Assembly* have called me.

My subject is *joy*, and in this I find comfort, for joy lightens the labor. You, Right Honorable Members, are the anointed of the Lord. By this, I mean you are set apart from your brethren for the great work of the Lord in this latter age of the world. On this day, a fresh anointing is poured out, and your hearts are to be filled with the oil of gladness for the work you have done—or rather, for what God has accomplished through you on our behalf. You have made Jerusalem rejoice, and God now calls you to rejoice with her. Yes, and all who love Jerusalem, who have mourned for her, must join in this day's rejoicing.

The tenth verse of Isaiah 66 is, as it were, the refrain at the end of a joyful song of praise. The reasons why all who love Jerusalem should rejoice are found beginning in verse five: "Hear the word of the LORD, ye that tremble at his word; Your brethren that hated you, that cast you out for my name's sake, said, Let the LORD be glorified: but he shall appear to your joy, and they shall be ashamed" (Isaiah 66:5). Therefore, we are commanded to "Rejoice with Jerusalem, and be glad for her, all ye that love her" (Isaiah 66:10). The passage continues: "A voice of noise from the city, a voice from the temple, a voice of the LORD that rendereth recompence to his enemies" (Isaiah 66:6). Further: "Before she travailed, she brought forth; before her pain came, she was delivered of a man child" (Isaiah 66:7). Then: "Who hath heard such a thing? who hath seen such things? Shall the earth be made to bring forth in one day? or shall a nation be born at once? for as soon as Zion travailed, she brought forth her children" (Isaiah 66:8). Finally: "Shall I bring to the birth, and not cause to bring forth? saith the LORD: shall I cause to bring forth, and shut the womb? saith thy God" (Isaiah 66:9). In light of all this, we *must rejoice* with Jerusalem, and all who mourn for her must rejoice with her.

Jerusalem's joy is *our* joy today. The reasons for her joy are also ours, as will become more evident as we continue our reflections. We are commanded to "Rejoice with Jerusalem," but let us apply this more personally: "Rejoice with England." Rejoice with the *church*. Is it possible? Shall England rejoice again? It was not long ago that God called us to mourning and weeping. Did we not cry out, "Woe unto us—the joy of our hearts is gone!"? We feared that even mercy was gone. Our peace was gone. The Gospel was gone. It seemed as if even our God had departed from us. Not long ago, we all felt the weight of sorrow. God's displeasure seemed like a dark cloud hanging heavily over our heads. Misgivings filled our hearts. Darkness surrounded us. Our harps were hung upon the willows. Some of us lamented, "How shall we sing the Lord's song in a strange land?" (Psalm 137:4). For though we were not captives of foreign enemies, we were driven into a *spiritual exile* by false friends and brethren in name only— "our brethren cast us out."

Others, still in their homeland, lamented, "How can we sing one of the Lord's songs even in our own land?" Such was the weight of oppression and the fears that gripped their hearts at home. But now behold! The Lord stands upon Mount Zion with His hundred and forty-four thousand, "having his Father's name written in their foreheads" (Revelation 14:1). They now boldly profess the name of the Lord, the truths of God, and the purity of His worship. They have taken their harps once more into their hands and sing a new song before the throne and before the elders (Revelation 14:3).

We are gathered this day to sing the song of praise to our God and to the Lamb before His throne and before you, our elders. Yes, together with you, God bids us to "Rejoice with Jerusalem, and be glad with her" (Isaiah 66:10). Let us rejoice! Let us sing together with one heart, lifting our voices to bless His holy name.

Rejoice! Let us all open our hearts to joy. God does not begrudge His people their joy. Rather, He desires that His people be glad with joy, that they leap for joy and be filled with it. "Rejoice evermore" (1 Thessalonians 5:16), rejoice in every circumstance. Yes, to be joyful in glory, to rejoice with joy unspeakable and full of glory (1 Peter 1:8), and to be transformed into joy itself—this God has promised to His people. As Isaiah 65:18 declares, "But be ye glad and rejoice for ever in that which I create: for, behold, I create Jerusalem a rejoicing, and her people a joy." Here the rejoicing is expressed in the abstract, emphasizing its fullness. God will exert His creative power rather than allow Jerusalem to remain without joy. Though He rejects the bread of mourners (Hosea 9:4), the joy of His people is pleasing to His soul. Therefore, let us now rejoice. The strength that might have been consumed in sorrow and distress, in fretting and vexation, let it now be drawn forth and spent in rejoicing before the Lord.

Part 2:
Rejoice with Jerusalem

Rejoice *with* Jerusalem—or rather, *for* Jerusalem. The very name "Jerusalem" means "Vision of Peace." Let us rejoice that today, England and Scotland can likewise be called a vision of peace—lands where we may now witness peace. Not long ago, we feared that we would see nothing but fire and the sword, bloodshed and devastation, confusion and darkness enveloping the land. You might have seen your homes burning, your children dashed against the stones, your wives and daughters ravished and slain before your eyes. Such are the unspeakable horrors that accompany war. But behold, instead of these dismal spectacles, we see a Jerusalem—a vision of peace. Today, we see and enjoy peace. Let us therefore rejoice and be glad for this, our Jerusalem.

Moreover, rejoice with Jerusalem not only as a vision of peace but as a *type* of the church. Rejoice in your outward peace, in the preservation of your estates, your liberties, your lives, and the safety of your families and friends. But above all, rejoice with and for Jerusalem—the church of God. Rejoice that we still have a church among us, that we still have the ordinances of God, the Gospel, and the Sabbath. You who love your lands, your pleasant homes, and your families, rejoice. But especially rejoice, you who love Jerusalem, the church of God.

The promise made to Abraham concerning his descendants was that they would be "as the sand which is upon the seashore" (Genesis 22:17)—numerous and earthly—and "as the stars of heaven" (Genesis 15:5)—numerous and spiritual. Indeed, Abraham's seed consists of both earthly and heavenly descendants. We all profess to be Abraham's seed. Some, however, are as the sand—earthly-minded and attached to the things below. Others are as the stars—heavenly-minded and raised above earthly desires. Yet all of us have reason to rejoice, for we have received the mercies of both heaven and earth.

There are many who delight in the peace and prosperity of the nation but give *little* thought to Jerusalem. They are excellent statesmen—wise, discerning, and faithful in their calling—yet they care little about the welfare of Jerusalem, the true worship of God. In Isaiah 8:2, we read of Uriah, who is called a "faithful witness," yet he was the same high priest who, when King Ahaz sent him a pattern of an altar he had seen in Damascus, built an altar like it and placed it in the temple of the Lord (2 Kings 16:10-16). Though Uriah was skilled and served faithfully in political matters, he was spiritually corrupt, conforming to idolatrous practices to please his superiors. Yet even if such men serve only as statesmen and care little for Jerusalem, they still have reason to rejoice in the outward peace. But none have as great a reason to rejoice, nor can any rejoice in a truly spiritual and acceptable manner, except those who love Jerusalem. Only those who stand with the Lamb on Mount Zion and who have His Father's name written on their foreheads can sing the song of praise described in Revelation 14:1-3: "And no man could learn that song but the hundred and forty and four thousand, which were redeemed from the earth." Our Jerusalem is from above, and only that part of Abraham's seed who are as the stars of heaven can or will sing the acceptable song of praise to the Lord this day.

You who love her—Jerusalem is lovely to the souls of the saints. "How amiable are thy tabernacles, O Lord of hosts!" (Psalm 84:1). Zion, the mount of Jerusalem, is described in Scripture as "the perfection of beauty" (Psalm 50:2). As the church enjoying the ordinances of God, Jerusalem is God's chosen portion—His pleasant portion, His dearly beloved. Upon Mount Zion is His throne of glory, His royal diadem, His crown jewel, His ornament of majesty. Such are the scriptural descriptions of the loveliness of Jerusalem. In Psalm 87:7, the psalmist declares, "All my springs are in thee," expressing the fullness of a heart overflowing with love for Jerusalem. Again, in Psalm 137:6, we read, "If I prefer not Jerusalem above my chief joy, let my right hand forget her cunning." What does it mean to prefer Jerusalem above one's "chief joy"? It literally means above "the head of my joy"—above the *highest* conceivable delight. If there is any joy higher than all others, Jerusalem must still be placed above it.

If you are truly gracious in spirit, the prosperity of Jerusalem will be a delight to your soul, for it fulfills your deepest desires. Therefore, rejoice with Jerusalem, you who love her. You may feel that you have done little for Jerusalem, or perhaps nothing at all. Yet if you love her, come to the feast of the Lord and rejoice. It is not only those who have rendered great service to Jerusalem who are called to rejoice—though, indeed, such service is the greatest honor and comfort a man can have under heaven. But you who love her, simply love her—come and rejoice with her this day.

There is, however, a generation of men who do *not* love Jerusalem. These men gnash their teeth in rage. They are filled with bitterness and frustration when they see her welfare. In Nehemiah 2:10, we read of Sanballat and Tobiah, who were "grieved exceedingly" when they heard that Nehemiah had come to seek the welfare of the children of Israel. How many Sanballats and Tobiahs do we have today, whose spirits are tormented because they see not just one man, but you—the worthies of our kingdom, the Honorable Assembly—seeking the welfare of Jerusalem? Psalm 59:6 compares the wicked to dogs: "They return at evening: they make a noise like a dog, and go round about the city." And in verse 14, we find a threat against them: in their vexation and madness at the prosperity of the saints, they will once again "go about the city, grinning like a dog." Not long ago, this scripture was fulfilled in the first sense, and today it is fulfilled in the latter.

I have read of tigers that are driven into a rage by aromatic scents that others find delightful. Likewise, we have had such "tigers" among us—men consumed by rage and cruelty against the saints. The sweet savor of their graces, so pleasing to God, enraged them. And now the sweet savor of the saints' peace, their liberties, and their comforts drives them into fresh fury. Yet we who love Jerusalem will not be moved by their malice. Instead, we will heed God's call to rejoice, for our joy in the Lord is secure and unshakable. Rejoice, therefore, with Jerusalem, you who love her!

Occumenius tells us that the fragrance of precious ointment is soothing and wholesome for doves, but it kills the beetle. We see the same contrast among people today. There is a great difference in how people perceive current events, as well as in the way their hearts respond to them. Yet, regardless of what others do, you who love Jerusalem—rejoice with her! Be glad! Our text says, *Rejoice with joy*. This phrase expresses a rich and pleasing emphasis, similar to what we read in Zephaniah 3:17, where God describes His own rejoicing over Jerusalem: "He will rejoice over thee with joy." God Himself rejoices with joy in His saints; let His saints also rejoice with joy in their God.

Rejoice, all you who mourn for her! Jerusalem was not long ago like a forsaken woman. Her children wandered through the streets mourning. Some even said that Jerusalem had turned into Babylon. They spoke of the ruin wrought among the saints—faithful ministers were taken away, ordinances were trampled upon, and truths were silenced. Those who were like pillars of the church were removed, and in their place, rotting posts and mere sticks were set up. Any truth or ordinance that promoted the power of godliness was especially targeted. If any saints were more distinguished, if any ministers were more faithful and useful, they were singled out for destruction. As Psalm 74:6 says, "But now they break down the carved work thereof at once with axes and hammers."

There was a time when the *adversaries* worked in secret, undermining the church little by little. But then they came openly with axes and hammers, using public violence, with no regard for the law. They struck hard and swiftly, determined to rid the land of the faithful altogether. The enemies of Jerusalem were great, and they prospered. Because of this, her children sighed and wept. They mourned together and shared their lamentations with one another. Their hearts were turned within them, but they found no comfort. Like doves, they mourned, hoping for justice but finding none. As Isaiah 59:11 says, "We roar all like bears, and mourn sore like doves: we look for judgment, but there is none."

But now, the time of mourning has passed. "Rejoice and be glad, rejoice with joy, all you who mourn for her." Your many fasting days for Jerusalem have now become joyful feasts. Come and gather the full harvest of joy—the fruit of the precious seed you sowed in tears. Come and see how God has treasured every tear you shed. Not one of them was lost upon the ground. They were all preserved by God and now bring forth joy. The more abundant your sowing in tears, the richer your harvest of joy. See how God has not only turned your water into wine but even your vinegar into wine.

Part 3: Doctrine

So far, I have only *introduced* the subject and provided a paraphrase of our text. But if we go deeper into it, we will discover three doctrinal truths:

1. Gracious hearts love Jerusalem, even when she is in a state of mourning.

2. God has appointed times to bring joy to those who mourn for His church.

3. When God brings mercy to Jerusalem, He calls His saints to rejoice and be glad with joy.

The first two points I will address briefly, but the third—being the most fitting for this occasion—deserves our extended attention.

Observation 1: Gracious hearts love Jerusalem, even in her mourning condition. It is no great thing to love Jerusalem when she is adorned in her glorious ornaments, when she shines with splendor in the eyes of all. But to love her when she is in affliction—when she is shrouded in mourning and surrounded by darkness—this is true and pure love. This is the love of the saints, as expressed in the words, "The zeal of thine house hath eaten me up" (John 2:17). This was spoken when the church was *in a troubled state.*

Consider Christ Himself: though He was "a man of sorrows, and acquainted with grief" (Isaiah 53:3), though there was "no beauty that we should desire him," He was still *altogether* lovely to the saints. The words of the Song of Songs 5:16 convey this perfectly: "His mouth is most sweet: yea, he is altogether lovely. This is my beloved, and this is my friend, O daughters of Jerusalem." To the saints, Christ is greater in His lowly stable than any emperor upon his throne. In the Latin words, "Major in stabulo Christus, quam in culmine imperii Augustus", meaning "Christ in the stable is greater than Augustus at the height of his empire."

Though Christ may be likened to a bundle of myrrh, bitter in taste yet fragrant, He is still the beloved of His church, lying close to her heart. As it is written in Song of Songs 1:13: "A bundle of myrrh is my well-beloved unto me; he shall lie all night betwixt my breasts." Myrrh symbolizes both sweetness *and* bitterness—just as Christ, though He endured suffering, remains precious and dear to His people.

This is the nature of the saints' love for Jerusalem. They love her in her mourning, when her beauty is marred and her splendor is dimmed, just as they love Christ in His suffering and humility. True love does not falter in times of affliction but remains steadfast, finding its highest expression when the beloved is *most* in need of comfort and care. Therefore, let us take this to heart as we continue to consider the joy that God now calls us to embrace. Rejoice, for God has remembered Jerusalem and comforted those who mourn for her.

Josephus tells us that when the Jews were *prosperous*, the Samaritans claimed to be of their blood. But in times of adversity, they *denied* any relation to them and disavowed any knowledge of their origin. This is how many people's hearts are toward Jerusalem. When the church flourishes, they can rejoice with her. But when she is in a state of mourning, they entertain vile thoughts about her. Yet, as the church is the dearly beloved of God's soul—even when she is given into the hands of her enemies—so she remains the dearly beloved of the saints' souls. As Jeremiah 12:7 says, "I have forsaken mine house, I have left mine heritage; I have given the dearly beloved of my soul into the hand of her enemies." Even when the church appears to lie low among the ruins, she is still like "a dove covered with silver, and her feathers with yellow gold" (Psalm 68:13).

Jerusalem was in a sorrowful condition when the ten tribes defected from Judah and from the true worship of God in Jerusalem, with the golden calves set up at Dan and Bethel as false centers of worship. Yet, even then, those with gracious hearts loved Jerusalem and risked great danger to travel there to worship the Lord in the true manner of His worship. In Hosea 5:1, we read, "Hear ye this, O priests; and hearken, ye house of Israel; and give ye ear, O house of the king; for judgment is toward you, because ye have been a snare on Mizpah, and a net spread upon Tabor." Mizpah and Tabor were located on the route from Samaria to Jerusalem, and they became places where traps were set to catch those who sought to go up to Jerusalem to worship. The priests themselves were described as the snare and the net. Either they personally ambushed the travelers or they instigated others to do so. They stirred up rulers and princes to lay hold of those traveling to Jerusalem. They even set spies to identify those who were determined to worship God according to His commands rather than content themselves with the false worship at Dan and Bethel. These faithful ones were met with derision and contempt. When Amaziah, the priest of Bethel, spoke to Amos, he scornfully said, "O thou seer, go, flee thee away into the land of Judah" (Amos 7:12). It was as if he meant, "Judah is the only place suitable for people as strict and precise as you. We in Bethel are not good enough for you. We are idolaters here—go to Judah, where you claim true worship is practiced." In this way, the true worship of God at Jerusalem, where the temple stood, was scorned, persecuted, and condemned.

    Yet, despite this opposition, those whose hearts were touched by God to seek Him remained faithful to Jerusalem. They would travel there to worship, no matter what they suffered for it. As we read in 2 Chronicles 11:16: "And after them out of all the tribes of Israel such as set their hearts to seek the LORD God of Israel came to Jerusalem, to sacrifice unto the LORD God of their fathers." Their love for Jerusalem endured, though it cost them dearly. Meanwhile, there were others who remained in Samaria, who perhaps wished things were different but would not risk anything to join the saints in the true worship of God at Jerusalem. But for those with spiritual hearts, the church's beauty could never be obscured by outward troubles. Her true glory shone through, even when she appeared blackened by affliction. As the bride says in Song of Songs 1:5, "I am black, but comely."

Recently, God put our love for Jerusalem to the test, for she was in a mournful state. What proof of love for her was there then? If your hearts were deceived by the outward decorations and false splendor of the "mother of fornications," the Roman Church—if your hearts were drawn away by the pomp and pageantry of Babylon—then you can find little comfort in what God has done and is still doing for Jerusalem in adorning her with *true* beauty. Now, in this time of peace, many "Parliamentary converts" have appeared—those who suddenly profess to love Jerusalem, flattering and fawning as though they have always supported her. But do not trust them! They have already revealed the duplicity of their hearts. They love their own appetites. They love their positions and possessions. But they do not love Jerusalem.

Josephus records that during Solomon's reign, when the nation of Israel flourished, the Jews were cautious about receiving proselytes, lest people come with self-serving motives, pretending to join themselves to the God of Israel for personal gain. This should be our wisdom today. Consider those who loved Jerusalem during her time of hardship, when such love was costly. Show them honor and respect. Encourage them. But toward those who now pretend to love Jerusalem, a discerning and cautious eye is needed. Do not regard them highly, for they may not truly seek the welfare of the church but rather their own advancement. Remember that true love for Jerusalem is not revealed in times of glory but in times of suffering. Those who have stood by her in her darkest days deserve our trust and our admiration.

But if our hearts have been sincere before God in loving Jerusalem in her sorrow, we can find comfort in the evidence of our genuine love for her and for God, who dwells in her. When Basil was criticized for standing by a friend during a time of danger, he replied, *Ego aliter amare non didici*—"I have not learned to love any other way." In *favorable* times, vermin creep out of their holes; in such times, it takes little grace to appear for God, for it is disgraceful not to do so. But to stand for Jerusalem when she is in mourning requires true love and steadfast faith.

Josephus records the sincere love of Herodias, Herod the Tetrarch's wife, for her husband in his time of affliction. When the Emperor banished Herod but offered Herodias her husband's estates because she was Agrippa's sister, she refused, saying, "There is a cause that hinders me from partaking of your bounty—namely, my love for my husband." She remained with Herod in his disgrace and exile. In the same way, the true spouse of Christ clings to Him and to His church in times of suffering. Her cry remains, "If I forget thee, O Jerusalem, let my right hand forget her cunning" (Psalm 137:5). Though Jerusalem may be in distress, the soul that loves her says, "If I forget thee..." God takes great pleasure in those who show love and respect to Jerusalem in her mourning state. He remembers their loyalty in times of adversity. He acknowledges their faithfulness, as He remembered Israel's devotion in the wilderness: "I remember thee, the kindness of thy youth, the love of thine espousals, when thou wentest after me in the wilderness, in a land that was not sown" (Jeremiah 2:2).

Consider how Solomon dealt with Abiathar the priest in 1 Kings 2:26. Though Abiathar deserved death, Solomon spared him, saying, "Thou art worthy of death: but I will not at this time put thee to death, because thou barest the ark of the Lord GOD before David my father, and because thou hast been afflicted in all wherein my father was afflicted." Abiathar's faithfulness during David's trials saved his life. In the same way, God regards those who have suffered alongside His church.

We also read of the kindness God showed to the Kenites because they had shown kindness to the Israelites during their journey from Egypt (Judges 1:16).

This mercy was extended to the Kenites over 400 years after their kindness to Israel. This shows that God remembers faithful love for generations.

True love that endures through affliction is love that will last forever. It was for this reason that David esteemed the men who stayed with him at Gath. They remained loyal during his time of hardship, and later, when David fled from Absalom, these same men went with him once more (2 Samuel 15:18). Their loyalty in times of trial bound them to David forever. Similarly, God honors those who stand with Jerusalem in her afflictions.

The *second* point is this: God has appointed times to turn the mourning of His saints for Jerusalem into rejoicing. He will not leave His people in the valley of Baca (the valley of weeping) forever; He will lead them to the valley of Beracah (the valley of blessing). In Ezekiel 9, we read that those who mourned for Jerusalem were marked for mercy. Similarly, Zephaniah 3:18 says, "I will gather them that are sorrowful for the solemn assembly, who are of thee, to whom the reproach of it was a burden." There was a time when the solemn assembly was despised, when *gathering for worship* brought persecution and ridicule. Many forsook it altogether. Yet the saints mourned for this reproach—it was a heavy burden on their hearts. God, however, promised that He would gather them in mercy. Though they had been scattered and exiled, they would be brought back.

In Exodus 24:10, we read that the elders of Israel "saw the God of Israel: and there was under his feet as it were a paved work of sapphire stone." Some interpreters understand this vision as a symbolic assurance that God would transform their condition—from sorrow and oppression to honor and joy. The bricks they made in slavery were now symbolically turned into sapphire. This reflects God's promise in Isaiah 54:11: "O thou afflicted, tossed with tempest, and not comforted, behold, I will lay thy stones with fair colors, and lay thy foundations with sapphires."

We also read in Revelation 11:3 of the two witnesses—faithful ministers of the Gospel—who prophesied in sackcloth during the thousand two hundred and sixty days of Antichrist's reign. The beast made war against them, overcame them, and killed them. Those who dwelt on the earth rejoiced over their deaths and made merry. But after a time, the witnesses stood upon their feet, and a voice from heaven said, "Come up hither." They ascended to heaven, and their enemies beheld them in awe. According to the scholar Mr. Meade, this resurrection occurred by the command of the supreme magistrate (*Magistratus Supremi jussu*). This aligns with the promise in Zechariah 12:5: "The governors of Judah shall say in their heart, The inhabitants of Jerusalem shall be my strength in the

LORD of hosts their God." There was a time when these leaders distrusted the faithful, viewing them as seditious, hypocritical, and troublesome. They believed the slander that these worshippers pretended to have special favor with God while being, in truth, the worst of men. But this perception will not last forever. The time will come when they will say in their hearts, "Our strength is in the inhabitants of Jerusalem." They will recognize that the saints are the most faithful of subjects, for their trust is in the Lord their God.

God will comfort His people. As Isaiah 40:1-3 says, "Comfort ye, comfort ye my people, saith your God. Speak ye comfortably to Jerusalem... Every valley shall be exalted." God will ensure that those who *mourn* for Jerusalem are *comforted*.

Reasons Why God Comforts the Mourners: 1. They are people of prayer. The mourners of Jerusalem are great in prayer, and great prayers yield great joy. Chrysostom compares this process to clouds that darken the heavens and cause gloomy weather. Yet, when those clouds release their rain, the skies become clear and the sunshine returns. In the same way, the sorrows and burdens in the hearts of the saints may seem dark and heavy, but when poured out before God in prayer, they become as sweet drops that bring forth the beams of His comforting love. When the saints have poured out their prayers and tears, God's gracious and comforting presence shines upon them, dispelling their gloom and filling their hearts with joy.

In this way, while sorrow may last for a night, joy comes in the morning. God's appointed time will come, and His saints, who have wept in prayer, will find themselves embraced by His love and lifted into His light.

2. Mourners are subject to much reproach. Those who mourn for Jerusalem *often* face scorn and derision. People mock them, calling them "whining Puritans" and accusing them of being constantly discontented with the times. The world cannot endure their sadness. In royal courts, no one is permitted to enter wearing sackcloth (Esther 4:2). Mourning garments and humility are considered out of place in the presence of earthly grandeur. The Hebrew word for *winter*—an emblem of affliction—also signifies *reproach*. Therefore, God delights in compensating such mourners with joy. Psalm 149:4 says, "For the LORD taketh pleasure in his people: he will beautify the meek with salvation." Their current sadness makes them despised and casts a shadow over them. But God will crown them with salvation and honor. Though they mourn in dishonor and are ridiculed by men, they shall one day be joyful in glory.

3. Christ is afflicted with His saints in all their afflictions: Isaiah 63:9 declares, "In all their affliction he was afflicted, and the angel of his presence saved them:

in his love and in his pity he redeemed them; and he bare them, and carried them all the days of old." Christ mourns alongside His people in all their sorrows. Surely, then, there must be a time for their rejoicing, for Christ's compassion compels Him to bring them comfort. Christ feels their grief because they suffer for His sake.

In Zechariah 12, we read of the great mourning at Hadadrimmon in the valley of Megiddo. This mourning was for Judah because King Josiah, who had joined Hadadrimmon in the fight against Pharaoh Necho, was slain in the battle. The lamentation was so bitter that it became proverbial, symbolizing the deep sorrow of a people mourning for one who suffered in their cause. If Hadadrimmon mourned Josiah with such grief, how much more will Christ, the King of kings, have compassion for those who suffer for Him? And if He has compassion, He will most certainly bring comfort.

Spiritual mourning purges and empties the heart, making it ready to receive the precious oil of God's mercies. As the saying goes, *Deus non infundit oleum misericordiae, nisi in vas contritum*— "God does not pour the oil of mercy except into a broken vessel." The heart must be *contrite* before it can be filled with the balm of *divine comfort*.

We have seen this fulfilled before our very eyes today—those who mourned and suffered have been comforted and honored.

A Call to Comfort the Mourners. Since this work of comforting mourners is one that God Himself undertakes, I beseech you, Right Honorable and beloved in Christ, to assist in this work. Do all that lies within your power to comfort those who have mourned for Jerusalem. It is a service most pleasing to the Lord. Allow me to speak plainly: you are deeply indebted to these faithful mourners, and justice requires that they receive both encouragement and support from you. Much of the good we now enjoy—our deliverance from the yoke of religious oppression and from the innovations imposed upon us—was made possible because of their steadfastness. Had none been willing to stand firm, to suffer for refusing illegal taxes and resisting corrupt religious practices, what would have become of us? Who were the ones who bore the burden of defending our religious liberties? Who stood up for the truth and endured reproach for the sake of God, their country, and their posterity? It was the mourners in Zion—the very ones who now deserve your comfort and esteem.

Others cared little for the fate of the church or the nation. They yielded to whatever was imposed upon them, even if it meant the enslavement of their estates, liberties, and consciences, simply to avoid any personal inconvenience. But these faithful ones bore the brunt of persecution. They suffered out of a conscientious duty to God and for the sake of future generations. Therefore, they deserve to be comforted and honored by you.

Blessed are you of the Lord for the work you have already done in this regard. The blessings of mourning hearts that you have gladdened rest upon you and your descendants—a benefit far greater than you can imagine. Blessed are you that you were born for such a time as this, to be made instruments of comfort to so many mourning saints of God. Chrysostom once said, "To show mercy is a more glorious work than to raise the dead." The kindness you show in relieving the oppressed and comforting the hearts of mourning saints is noted by God. These saints, whom you have comforted, daily lift their prayers to their Father, telling Him of your mercy and compassion. Christ will not forget this service. On the day of judgment, He will say, "Come, ye blessed of my Father... for I was hungry, and ye gave me meat: I was thirsty, and ye gave me drink: I was a stranger, and ye took me in... I was in prison, and ye came unto me" (Matthew 25:34-36).

Therefore, continue *steadfastly* in this work, for in comforting the mourners, you not only bring joy to them—you honor Christ Himself. And in honoring Christ, you secure for yourselves and your posterity the blessings of heaven. Let your hands not grow weary in this labor of love, for great is your reward.

Part 4:
The Third Doctrine

The third point—the primary doctrine intended in the text and most fitting for our present work—is this, *doctrine: when God bestows mercy upon Jerusalem, He calls His saints to rejoice and be glad with joy.*

David, in Psalm 106:6, expresses his desire to witness "the good of thy chosen," and for what purpose? "That I may rejoice in the gladness of thy nation, that I may glory with thine inheritance." The goodness shown to God's chosen should lead to rejoicing, gladness, and glorying in His name.

Throughout the book of Revelation, we observe this pattern of joy and triumph whenever God displays His mercies toward His church. In Revelation 4:8-9, the heavenly host cries out, "Holy, holy, holy, Lord God Almighty, which was, and is, and is to come." They give glory, honor, and thanks to Him who sits upon the throne and lives forever. Similarly, in chapter 7:9-12, a great multitude appears with white robes and palms in their hands, crying out, "Salvation to our God which sitteth upon the throne, and unto the Lamb… Blessing, and glory, and wisdom, and thanksgiving, and honor, and power, and might, be unto our God forever and ever." Again, in chapter 19:6, the voices of a great multitude are likened to the sound of many waters and mighty thunderings, proclaiming, "Alleluia: for the Lord God omnipotent reigneth."

This rejoicing over the mercies of God toward Jerusalem is a vital part of walking with God. What does it mean to walk with God? It means observing the direction of His providence, following where He leads in His special works toward His saints, and aligning our hearts accordingly. We mourn when He calls for mourning, and we rejoice when He commands us to rejoice. Surely, God Himself rejoices more in the welfare of Jerusalem than in the entire world besides.

Alvarez, commenting on Isaiah 66:9, reflects on God's declaration, "Shall I bring to the birth, and not cause to bring forth?" He notes that, in comparison, God considers all His works as insignificant unless they result in good for Jerusalem. If this is true, we are called to make Jerusalem's welfare the supreme object of our joy.

In Jerusalem, the glory of God's presence is revealed. When He builds up Zion, He appears in His glory (Psalm 102:16). His name is magnified: "In Judah is God known: his name is great in Israel" (Psalm 76:1). In Jerusalem, God establishes His public worship in the great ordinances where He displays His glory most fully and graciously. There, He commands the blessing—even life forevermore (Psalm 133:3). Consider these aspects of His blessing:

1. It is His blessing—God's personal and deliberate favor.
2. It is "the blessing"—a particular, choice blessing.
3. It is life, even life forevermore—a blessing that endures for eternity.
4. It is a commanded blessing—a powerful decree that cannot be thwarted.
5. It comes from Zion—the appointed place of God's favor.

Psalm 134:3 says, "The Lord that made heaven and earth bless thee out of Zion." Notice that the psalmist does not say, "Bless thee out of the earth," though God made both heaven and earth. Instead, he emphasizes *Zion*, as though the blessings that come from there surpass all other blessings from heaven and earth.

Fulfillment of Prophecy and Cause for Rejoicing. When Jerusalem prospers, prophecies are fulfilled, and the hearts of the saints are filled with joy. The revelation of prophecies concerning the welfare of the church is itself a great blessing and a reason for rejoicing. Revelation 5:1-4 describes how John wept when he saw the sealed book that no one could open. But then the Lamb appeared, "as it had been slain" (Revelation 5:6), and He opened the book, revealing the mysteries that concerned the church. A learned interpreter observes that this privilege—the opening of the prophecies—was *purchased* by the blood of Christ. Before His death, Christ did not reveal these things in the same way; they were disclosed as a direct result of His sacrifice. When the prophecies were opened, there was *immediate* rejoicing. The elders took their harps and golden vials full of incense and sang a new song (Revelation 5:8-9). Every creature in heaven and earth joined in praise: "Blessing, and honor, and glory, and power, be unto him that sitteth upon the throne, and unto the Lamb for ever and ever" (Revelation 5:13).

If it is such a cause for joy to have the prophecies concerning Jerusalem's good revealed, how much greater is the joy when those prophecies are fulfilled!

The Vindication of God's Cause and the Honor of His Saints. When Jerusalem prospers, prayers are answered. "Let the heart of them rejoice that seek the Lord" (Psalm 105:3). How much more should the hearts of those who *find* the Lord rejoice! In Jerusalem's triumph, the truths of God are vindicated, and the saints are honored. This is a time of great rejoicing. Reflecting on what God has done for His church in the past is cause for joy, but even more so is partaking in His present mercies. Psalm 66:6 recalls how God "turned the sea into dry land: they went through the flood on foot: there did we rejoice in him."

A Great Year of Mercies. Let this day remind you to enlarge your hearts with joy and gratitude for the mercies we have received. If I were to attempt to recount all the mercies of God that call for our rejoicing, there would *be no end*. David appointed certain Levites to minister before the ark of the Lord, to record and give thanks and praise for Israel's mercies. Likewise, we must not forget the mercies bestowed upon us this year.

You have already heard a catalogue of these mercies this morning, but let me speak briefly again: This year has been a year of wonders for England and Scotland. It was once said of the year 1588, "*Octogesimus octavus mirabilis annus*"— "the wondrous year of eighty-eight." But we may say even more of this year, "*Quadragesimus primus mirabilis annus*"— "the wondrous year of forty-one."

God has shown great honor to this nation, for it has stood for the cause of religion and conscience against the Antichristian powers. This was never an act of rebellion against the king—on the contrary, the king himself has acknowledged the loyalty of these defenders. They have sought to uphold his honor while maintaining true religion and purging the land of superstition and tyranny.

The Honor of a Peaceful Departure. Even in times of hostility, these faithful ones retained peace in their hearts. They conducted themselves honorably and departed from us in peace. This great work of the Lord has become a cause for admiration among the surrounding nations. Many cried out against them, accusing them of hypocrisy and greed, saying, "They only pretend to care about religion; they seek only to stir up strife and plunder our estates." But they were wrong—God Himself has vindicated their innocence.

Their example is unparalleled in the annals of history. Never before has an army, holding such strategic positions and enduring such hardship, conducted itself with such justice and peace. Though they could have sought relief through unjust means, they chose instead to suffer for righteousness' sake. When they finally departed, they blessed the people and prayed for them.

A Model for All Congregations. Let their example be proclaimed in all the congregations of England today. God has caused their adversaries to bow before them, proving that He is with those who stand for His truth. Let us, therefore, rejoice in the mercies of God toward His church, for they testify to His faithfulness, His power, and His unwavering love. May our hearts be filled with gratitude, and may our praises rise to Him who sits upon the throne and unto the Lamb forever and ever.

Master Brightman, in his commentary on the book of Revelation, many years ago, compared the Church of Scotland to the church of Philadelphia. To that church, God made a promise: He would cause those who claimed to be Jews but were not to bow before her and acknowledge that He had loved her. How marvelously has God fulfilled this promise for them!

Those who once declared themselves to be true members of the church and cried out, "The church, the church," as though they alone labored for her, but who in reality were not true members at all, have now been compelled to bow down. Everyone can see that God has loved them. If the honoring of one individual and the vindication of his innocence is cause for rejoicing, how much more is the honoring of an entire nation and the clearing of its integrity cause for praise? Let others vex themselves and fret as they will, but let those who love Jerusalem rejoice, be glad, and give praise to God this day.

Moreover, this year is truly a *"mirabilis annus"*—a wonderful year—in that it so closely resembles the day of judgment. We now see the goats on the left hand and the sheep on the right. Never in our time, nor in the time of our forefathers, have we witnessed such a clear representation of the day of judgment in our nation.

What shall I say about the confirmation of our hopes—the continued enjoyment of our liberties, the peace of our consciences, and the preservation of the truth of our religion—through the establishment of the Triennial Parliament? God indeed opened a door of hope, yet the guilt upon the land made us fear its closing almost every day. But now, to strengthen our weakness, God has secured this door with a bar to keep it from being shut. Oh, let us rejoice this day for this great mercy of our God and give Him the praise He is due!

Part 5:
Reasons of Jerusalem's Joy

There is yet one more mercy—though mentioned this morning—that deserves to be repeated again and again for the praise of our God and the rejoicing of the saints: that our representative kingdom and the nation itself have entered into an oath and covenant with the Lord to defend His truth against popery and its corruptions. "All you who love Jerusalem, rejoice at this! Be glad and rejoice with joy!" For a kingdom to enter into a covenant with God—oh, how sweet and acceptable a sacrifice this is!

Let us consider the reasons for Jerusalem's joy as drawn from the context of the text. Isaiah 66:5 declares: "Hear the word of the Lord, ye that tremble at his word; Your brethren that hated you, that cast you out for my name's sake, said, Let the Lord be glorified: but he shall appear to your joy, and they shall be ashamed." Among us, there have been many who trembled at the Word of the Lord, recognizing its dreadful authority and God's jealousy concerning His worship. Their hearts stood in awe of His Word. They dared not act as others did, no matter the pressures from men in authority, no matter how pompous the practices or how many learned men endorsed them. Their hearts were overawed by the Word of God. These men were persecuted and condemned. Their trembling before God's Word was labeled as obstinacy and pride, and this was used as an excuse to oppress their tender consciences.

The mindset of the oppressors was this, "We know what scruples trouble their consciences. Let us press them exactly where they are most tender." This was their strategy: "If they are content with the ceremonies of old, let us introduce new ones—they will surely resist those." When some yielded to certain innovations, the oppressors devised further schemes: "They will scruple at the new declaration of sports on Sundays—let us make it mandatory." And when this failed to break them, they turned to the oath *ex officio* and charged them with crimes, regardless of their innocence. Their ultimate goal was to ensnare the saints by forcing them to take an oath that would bind their consciences.

Such exploitation of tender consciences is the most cursed, hellish oppression that could ever enter the heart of man. To determine where men's consciences are most sensitive and to compel them there unto the utmost—oh, how the heavens must shudder at such wickedness! How the earth must groan beneath it! I believe no nation in the world has ever seen an oppression of conscience to parallel what was practiced here in England. But now God has appeared for the honor and joy of those who trembled at His Word. These faithful ones were *willing* to part with their possessions, their estates, their homes, and even their freedom *rather than* act against the Word of God.

Part 5: Reasons of Jerusalem's Joy

Rejoice, You Who Love Jerusalem. "Your brethren that hated you cast you out." They pretended to be your brethren and addressed you as such, but in their hearts, they despised you. Their rage was unrelenting: "Let their families be ruined. Let them starve. Let them rot in prison." What did it matter to them, so long as they themselves could live in luxury, adorned with pomp, and reveling in merriment with their overflowing cups? They cast you out—out of their churches, out of their society, out of their hearts. They denied you civil and religious liberties, not for any fundamental differences, but for issues of conscience in matters indifferent or disputable. I speak modestly when I say this—it is sinful to cast out any whom Christ has not cast out. We must receive all whom Christ receives and cast out none except those whom He has already rejected. But now, rejoice, for God has begun to gather the outcasts of Israel. He will gather them in mercy.

God's Vindication. The Lord has heard the cries of the oppressed and has graciously acted on their behalf. The very ones who cast you out are now forced to recognize the hand of God upon you. The Lord has shown that His favor rests upon you, not upon them. Those who mocked and scorned you, who derided your scruples and branded your consciences as weak, are now ashamed. God has justified His saints before the eyes of all.

The outcasts are being restored. Just as God promises to gather His people in Isaiah 11:12—"He shall set up an ensign for the nations, and shall assemble the outcasts of Israel, and gather together the dispersed of Judah from the four corners of the earth"—so too is He gathering His faithful ones *today*. Therefore, let us rejoice and be glad, for the Lord has done marvelous things. He has turned the shame of His people into honor, their mourning into dancing, and their reproach into praise. Let all who love Jerusalem lift their voices in thanksgiving and declare the greatness of our God. Let us proclaim His faithfulness from generation to generation, for His mercy endures forever.

"They cast you out for my name's sake." They accused you of being seditious, rebellious, and disobedient to authority. But I, the Lord, will own your cause—it was for *my* name's sake. I, who know your hearts, declare that what you did was out of obedience to me. Though there may have been some weakness mixed in, I will still own it as being for *my* name's sake. God names things *differently* than men do. What the world calls faction, God calls faithfulness. What will it profit you, who cast reproachful titles on the saints and their ways, when God Himself gives them new and honorable names? What you call "faction" or "stubbornness," God calls service done for His name's sake.

Let God Be Glorified—Three Interpretations. 1. A False Pretense of Piety. Those who cast out the saints often claim to be acting for God's glory. "We are working for the honor of Christ," they say, "for the peace of the church. We desire that God's worship be conducted decently and in order." They boast of their public spirit and their desire to promote religion and increase its respectability in the world. However, glorious ends are often used to conceal the vilest actions. It is one of the worst forms of persecution when men sincerely believe they are doing God a service by *harming His people*. One of the fiercest persecutions in the early church occurred under the Roman Emperor Trajan, who was reputed for his integrity but was relentless in persecuting Christians, thinking he was preserving justice. Let all who hear these words take heed not to cloak their ambitions in the language of religion. Do not pursue church unity or peace in ways that God will not approve of or thank you for in the end. Be wary lest, while pretending to glorify God, you instead strike at His honor and wound Him by harming His people. Just as Oedipus unknowingly killed his father, believing him to be his enemy, so too are Christ and His church often wronged by those who think they are defending Him.

2. *A Mockery of the Saints.* "Let God be glorified" can also be an expression of mockery and derision. "Oh, you are so strict and precise! You act as though you alone care about God's glory, as though no one else has a

conscience or a soul to save." The saints of God have long been mocked for their godliness, especially in the courts of the great and powerful. "What?" they sneer, "Your conscience forbids you? The glory of God—that is what you hide behind! You won't do what we all do, what learned men approve of?" These taunts and jeers have often been directed at the most godly, by spirits who regard humility and godly fear as weakness and hypocrisy.

3. *A Challenge to God's Power.* Finally, "Let God be glorified" can be read as a challenge: "If you truly belong to God, let Him deliver you. Let us see if God will uphold your cause. If your claim is righteous, why doesn't He appear for you?" Just as the Pharisees mocked Christ on the cross, saying, "He trusted in God; let him deliver him now, if he will have him" (Matthew 27:43), so too have the saints been scorned and oppressed by those who ask why God does not rescue them. The oppressors grow emboldened when they prosper in their ways, while the saints seem abandoned. They take comfort in the approval of the powerful and the lack of opposition. They bless themselves, convinced of their righteousness because they seem to flourish. In the meantime, the saints mourn, cry out to heaven, and weep over their sufferings, asking, "How long, O Lord, holy and true? When wilt Thou appear to maintain Thine own cause?" But now—God *has* appeared! "Rejoice with Jerusalem,

all you who love her," for the Lord has shown Himself mighty on behalf of His servants.

God's Vindication and the Saints' Triumph. The saints have waited upon the Lord in patience, and now they triumph in His salvation. As Isaiah 25:9 proclaims, "Lo, this is our God; we have waited for him, and he will save us: this is the LORD; we have waited for him, we will be glad and rejoice in his salvation." God has appeared when no one else would stand for His people. How many were afraid to stand with the suffering saints? When one deer in a herd is wounded, the others push it away, leaving it to fend for itself. So too did many push the suffering saints away, reluctant to associate with them. How many failed to appear when the saints needed them most, fearful of losing their position or reputation! "The Lord lay not this great sin to their charge."

But though men did not appear, *God* did. When there was no human deliverer, God's own arm brought salvation (Isaiah 59:16). Blessed be our God, who has not caused the expectation of His people to fail. It is He who has appeared! Our condition was such that only God Himself could bring deliverance. When we looked to human means, we saw no way forward. Yet as Abraham discovered on Mount Moriah, "In the mount of the Lord it shall be seen" (Genesis 22:14). And indeed, on the mountain, the Lord has been seen! "Rejoice with Jerusalem, all you who love her!"

God Appeared Sooner Than Expected. We believed and hoped that God would one day vindicate His people, but few of us expected to see it in our own time. That He has appeared so swiftly, even within our days, is beyond our greatest hopes and expectations. He has appeared to our joy, glorifying His own name. Those things which were once despised—truth, purity, and humble faith—are now honored. Many who once opposed true religion are now earnestly seeking the way of Christ's government in His church and striving to purge His worship from superstition and corruption. In this, God has gloriously appeared to our joy. "Oh, rejoice with Jerusalem, all you who love her!"

The Saints Lift Up Their Faces. God has put honor upon His servants. They now lift up their heads with joy, while their adversaries hang their heads in shame, dejected and disappointed. God has justified His saints and put an honor upon godliness itself. It is no longer a reproach to be zealous in the ways of God. Those who desire to walk closely with God find encouragement from leaders like you, Right Honorable, whose example is watched by the entire kingdom.

What God has begun to do among us, we trust, is only the beginning of the great work He intends to accomplish in this latter age—to raise up Jerusalem as "a praise in the earth" (Isaiah 62:7). He has appeared, and He has appeared gloriously. Therefore, "Rejoice with Jerusalem, all you who love her! Be glad for her and rejoice with joy!" Let your hearts be full of thanksgiving, for the Lord has done great things for His church. Let us praise His name, for His mercy endures forever.

"And they shall be ashamed." They sought to cast shame upon the saints, vilifying and reproaching them as much as they could, trampling them underfoot as *though* they were worthless dirt. Oh, how shamefully were men of noble and godly spirit treated in the courts of unjust authority, humiliated by every petty commissary! What vile names they were called by men who were unworthy even to sit with the dogs of the flock! But now, who has become vile in the eyes of all? Who are the ones despised and loathsome to the people? God has fulfilled His Word. As it is written in Malachi 2:8-9: "Ye are departed out of the way; ye have caused many to stumble at the law... therefore have I also made you contemptible and base before all the people, according as ye have not kept my ways, but have been partial in the law."

I need not name who these people are—those who have *corrupted the covenant*, who have twisted Scripture to suit their ambitions and turned it against the godly to sadden the hearts of those whom God intended to comfort. In righteous judgment, God has made them vile before the people. Though they rage and fret because of it, they fail to recognize that it is *God's* hand that has humbled them. It is the Lord who has made them contemptible.

God's declaration in Revelation 3:16, "I will spew thee out of my mouth," has been strikingly fulfilled. Consider it well—what generation of men in England today weighs upon the hearts and stomachs of the people, ready to be cast out? I do not need to name them; they are so loathed that it seems all that remains is for the finger to be placed on the throat—and they will be expelled. There is a readiness in the spirit of the nation to cast them off, and God will accomplish it in His time. We trust and hope that this time is at hand.

A Failure to See God's Majesty. "They shall be ashamed, yet they will not see the majesty of the Lord; Lord, when thy hand is lifted up, they will not see: but they shall see, and be ashamed for their envy at the people" (Isaiah 26:10-11). These men have despised the common people, treating them as if their very souls existed solely to be trampled upon. Yet now they shall be ashamed "for their envy at the people."

Since God has acted so decisively for the shame of His enemies, "let all who love Jerusalem rejoice with her" and praise the great God who has governed all things so graciously and wonderfully.

A Voice from the City and the Temple. Isaiah 66:6 continues, "A voice of noise from the city, a voice from the temple, a voice of the Lord that rendereth recompense to his enemies." Some interpret this as referring to the voice heard in the temple before the destruction of Jerusalem—a cry of doom: "*Migremus hinc*— "Let us be gone!" *"Ite ad Pellam"*— "Get to Pella!" This voice of noise represents the tumult and terror of judgment, particularly the noise of war that shook the temple, striking terror in the hearts of the people. They would not heed God's voice in His Word, spoken through His messengers; it was to them nothing more than noise. But now they will hear another voice—one of terror, a noise of war, bringing recompense to God's enemies. Yet, this judgment will not come near the saints. "No green thing shall be hurt" (Revelation 9:4). Though it is but the sound of war, it carries divine recompense for the enemies of God's people.

Even though, in mercy, God has prevented much shedding of blood, the very *threat* of war has served as recompense for His enemies. No people have been more frustrated and disappointed than they. Though there has been no outright battle, God's voice of war has confounded them and shattered their plans. Many of them longed for war in their bitterness, hoping to regain their lost positions and satisfy their insatiable lusts. They would gladly have seen their neighbor's house burned if only their own "egg" could be roasted by the fire. Yet, their desires have been thwarted. God's time for recompense upon His people's adversaries has come.

That Rendereth Recompense. And how has God recompensed them? Measure for measure—scorn for scorn, shame for shame, loss for loss. Those who deprived faithful ministers of their homes and possessions have themselves suffered loss. Those with blood on their hands have seen blood come upon them. Two scriptures, in particular, have been fulfilled upon the adversaries of God's people:

    1. Exodus 18:11: "In the thing wherein they dealt proudly, He was above them."

    2. Psalm 9:16: "The wicked is snared in the work of his own hands."

Higgain Selah—think deeply upon this. These two Hebrew words are placed together *only* here, underscoring the importance of reflecting on God's righteous work so that He may receive glory. In Revelation 15:3, the saints sing praise to God for His judgments: "Great and marvelous are thy works, Lord God Almighty; just and true are thy ways, thou King of saints." God's judgments are not only great and marvelous but also just and true. Therefore, "Rejoice with Jerusalem, all you who love her."

    The Voice of Judgment from Church and State. "A voice from the city, a voice from the temple." This signifies that both the civil and ecclesiastical realms now align with God's work of recompense. Corruption was rampant in both the church and the state. Idols had been set up in Dan and Bethel—one representing judgment (Dan) and the other the house of God (Bethel). Judgment itself had been corrupted, and the house of God defiled. But now, the voice of judgment arises from both city and temple against the corrupt.

In our own time, we can see a similar pattern. A voice has come from the city—a petitioning voice, graciously received by you. A voice has also come from the temple—a plea from the faithful to render recompense to the enemies of God's church. Oh, that the ministry's voice would always be united, so that you would not be distracted by differing messages! Division in the church creates confusion. Augustine, in his time, lamented the bitter disputes among church leaders, saying: *Prociderem ad pedes*—"I would fall at their feet to beg them for unity." Such divisions existed between Chrysostom and Epiphanius, between Jerome and Rufinus, between Luther and Oecolampadius. But be not disheartened, you worthies of the Lord. Despite the many voices, there is still the *voice of the Lord*. It is His voice that will prevail, guiding you amidst all the clamor.

Blessed be God that His voice has been the determining voice among you! It has directed your spirits beyond human wisdom. Despite the conflicting voices, God's voice has led you in a blessed and wise way, bringing *glory* to His name.

Part 6:
A Call to Rejoice

"Rejoice therefore with Jerusalem, all you who love her; be glad and rejoice with joy." God has silenced the enemies, lifted up His saints, and shown Himself mighty in their defense. The honor of the righteous has been restored. Let us, therefore, lift up our hearts in praise. Let all who love Jerusalem rejoice and glorify the Lord for His righteous judgments and His marvelous works. His mercy endures forever, and His faithfulness is from generation to generation.

Isaiah 66:7 declares, "Before she travailed, she brought forth; before her pain came, she was delivered of a man child." This verse describes a miraculous mercy—deliverance without the expected anguish of labor.

If we had received this mercy after long travail and suffering, we would have counted it as a great recompense, well worth enduring the hardships. Even those who had the highest hopes for mercy in England believed that severe judgment would precede it. We fully expected that we would pass through a furnace of affliction, through fire and water, before being brought into the "wealthy place" God prepared for us. We assumed the path would be soaked with much blood. Yet God, in His mercy, has prevented our fears and surpassed our hopes, for "before she travailed, she brought forth."

Consider how long Germany has travailed in war, with her blood pouring out horribly in her travail, yet she has not yet brought forth. But God has been merciful to England—before her travail, she brought forth! Oh, "rejoice with Jerusalem for this!" This is a mercy indeed—an extraordinary mercy—deliverance from the horrors of rolling in blood, from civil war, from the horrors of nation rising against nation. We scarcely understand the full worth of this mercy.

The Horror of War. I recall reading about the people of Numantia, a city besieged by the enemy. Unable to hold out any longer, the young and strong men of the city gathered the old men, women, and children and slew them. They piled all the city's riches into the marketplace, set it aflame, and watched everything burn. Finally, each of them took poison and perished in one day—all this to avoid falling into the hands of their enemies. Such was their dread of being overtaken by the devouring sword.

War—especially civil war—brings untold terror. For us, such a war would have been even more dreadful, considering how long we have enjoyed peace. Long-standing peace has softened our spirits. We have no fortified towns to retreat to for refuge, as they have in other countries. How terrifying would such a prospect be! Even now, though we are delivered from it, the very thought of war strikes horror into our hearts.

Had the tragedy of widespread bloodshed occurred, imagine someone asking, "For what cause is all this?" And if the only answer had been, "For the defense of a bishop's rochet, a surplice, or a cross," how sad and grievous that would have been! If the war had truly been about defending the king's honor and lawful rights, that would have been a cause worthy of sacrificing our lives. But it has become evident that the blood that would have been shed was loyal blood. And what a pity it would have been to spill it! The people of this land, loyal and committed, have been willing to lay down their lives to uphold the king's lawful rights.

But had war broken out, what would the war's title have been? Surely it would have been known as an Episcopal Bellum—an Episcopal war. And have the Prelatical Party deserved so well at our hands that we should venture our peace, our estates, and our blood for their defense? No matter the outcome of such a war, it would have been disastrous for us. If the sword had prevailed on their side, it would have been drenched in the blood of our wives and children—a tragedy recorded in infamy for generations. And if we had prevailed, we would have been stained with the blood of our brethren. Besides the guilt upon our souls, what would we have gained if the Prelatical Party had been restored to power? What could we have expected but new superstitious innovations, more illegal practices, and deeper bondage of our estates, liberties, and consciences? To risk our estates and spill the blood of our brethren for that victory—how miserable would that have been?

A nation is in a grievous state when war threatens at its gates, and yet even victory would mean ruin. But blessed be God—we have been delivered from this dire condition! "Rejoice with Jerusalem, all you that love her; be glad and rejoice with joy."

The Misuse of Religious Zeal. It is true that all illegal tumults and outbreaks must be condemned and suppressed. Yet, if those who are contemptuously labeled "Puritans" had been the true cause of such disturbances, such unbearable burdens to the kingdom, they would hardly have been able to walk the streets without being stoned. Therefore, instead of fretting and lamenting about disorder, the Prelatical Party ought to bless God that things are as calm and peaceful as they are.

Mercy without travail. Well, mercy has indeed come to us, and the pains of travail we feared have not come upon us. We expected to be cast into severe affliction and devastation, yet God has prevented it. He has shown that He can bring about deliverance without the dreadful labor we anticipated. While others in history have suffered unspeakably for their deliverance, God, in His goodness, has spared us.

Had civil war consumed this land, it would have been unbearable, especially for a people unaccustomed to hardship and softened by long peace. But God, in His gracious providence, has brought forth mercy swiftly, sparing us from the terror of war and the shedding of innocent blood. Therefore, "Rejoice with Jerusalem, all you that love her; be glad and rejoice with joy!" Let us lift our hearts in praise to God, who has delivered us from destruction and crowned us with peace.

Jeremiah 46:16 tells of those who said, "We will go to our own people, to the land of our birth, from the oppressing sword." Yet, for us exiles, this was not possible for a time. Instead, we feared returning to our homeland, lest we encounter the sword. But now, by the mercy of God, we have returned and found peace and safety. Here, instead of oppression, we have met with the voice of joy and gladness. Your homes, arms, and hearts are opened wide to receive us. We scarcely believed we would ever see our homeland again. And now, behold, we are here—gathered with our honorable senators and the worthies of our nation, called by them to rejoice with them and to praise our God in the great congregation. "Who is like unto Thee, O Lord?" The mercies of God are beyond measure. "Great and marvelous are thy works, O Lord God Almighty; who would not fear thee?" The Lord is truly God, "the Lord is God!"

Mercy Instead of Bloodshed. In Joel 3:10, we read of times when men are called to "beat their plowshares into swords, and their pruning hooks into spears." We feared this would be our fate. But instead, through God's abundant mercy, we have seen the promise of Isaiah 2:4 fulfilled: "They shall beat their swords into plowshares, and their spears into pruning hooks."

This mercy is the fulfillment of the promise in Isaiah 9:5, where God speaks of victory "without confused noise, and without garments rolled in blood." Such a mercy is ours now. If Christ had come upon His red horse, with garments dyed in blood, to claim His kingdom by force, we would still have rejoiced in His reign. But instead, He has come to us upon His white horse, bearing mercy and peace. What cause for rejoicing this is!

While our brethren may have believed we were sweltering in our own blood, here we sit beneath our vines and fig trees, basking in the beams of God's mercy.

Our Deliverance—The Fruit of Christ's Travail: we have been delivered without the pains of travail—but this mercy is the *fruit* of Christ's travail. Our blood has been spared because of the blood He shed. We must view even outward deliverances as the fruits of Christ's sacrifice. Zechariah 9:11 speaks to this: "As for thee also, by the blood of thy covenant I have sent forth thy prisoners out of the pit wherein is no water." We may say the same of England. By the blood of the covenant, the pit has not consumed us.

The Power of Prayer. This deliverance from the travail we feared has also come through the travail of the saints in prayer. How many cried to heaven: "If it be possible, let this cup pass from us! O Lord, if it be possible, let this cup of blood pass from us!" And the Lord has heard those cries. The cup of blood has passed from us, and in its place, behold—a cup of salvation!

Let us, therefore, receive it with thanksgiving and joy and praise the name of the Lord our God forever. Surely, prayer has been the midwife that helped bring forth this mercy. This is why the pains of travail have been so light.

What Has Been Brought Forth? But what has been brought forth? If a birth occurs without pain, and yet what is born is feeble, mean, or worthless, there is little cause for rejoicing. But this is no such case. What has been brought forth is a man-child—a strong and vigorous mercy that immediately crushes the "Babylonish brats" of innovations that were newly hatched. This mercy promises great blessings for us. It is a mercy of immense consequence, glorious in our eyes and in the eyes of all the surrounding nations.

A Glorious Contrast. Consider the lament of the church in Isaiah 26:17-18: "As a woman with child, that draweth near the time of her delivery, is in pain, and crieth out in her pangs; so have we been in thy sight, O

Lord. We have been with child, we have been in pain, we have as it were brought forth wind; we have not wrought any deliverance in the earth."

How different is our situation now! They travailed in great pain and brought forth nothing but wind. But we, though spared the pains of travail, have brought forth a man-child—a glorious deliverance in this land! This mercy is a foundation for future generations and a blessing not only to us but to the entire Christian world.

A Mercy Without Parallel. This mercy is unparalleled by any mercy England has received since the Gospel first came to these shores. God has done such things through you—our honorable leaders—as show the magnanimity and true heroism of your spirits. For this, your names will be blessed for generations to come. In this latter age, God is raising His glorious name in the world, setting His King upon His holy hill and making Jerusalem a *praise* in all the earth. What has already been accomplished is but a preparation for and a foretaste of this great and glorious work. Blessed are the men whom God uses as instruments for this purpose.

The Fall of Babylon. The greatest blow ever dealt to Antichristian government has been struck in this time. "Babylon is fallen, is fallen," (Revelation 14:8), and fallen so utterly that it will *never* rise again in power. We now hear a noise not only from many waters but from thunder, proclaiming: "Hallelujah! The Lord God omnipotent reigneth!" (Revelation 19:6). The voice from many waters represents the cries of the people. For a time, their cries were dismissed and condemned. But the voice of thunder—the voice of those in places of dignity and power—is unmistakable and terrifying to the adversaries. Now the voices of the people and the leaders are joined together in praising God for His righteous reign.

A Call to Rejoice. Therefore, let all who love Jerusalem rejoice with her. Let us give thanks for this extraordinary mercy—a deliverance beyond our expectations, wrought not through blood and anguish, but through the grace of God and the prayers of His saints. Let us remember that this mercy, born without the pain of travail, is no weak or insignificant blessing but a mighty, vigorous gift from God. It is the beginning of something greater—the raising of Jerusalem as the praise of the whole earth. Let us, therefore, rejoice and be glad. "The Lord God omnipotent reigneth!" May His name be glorified forever, for His mercy endures to all generations.

In Revelation 12:1, John speaks of "a woman clothed with the sun, and the moon under her feet." A learned interpreter has noted that the "moon" represents ceremonial rites, not merely the world or temporal things, because the Jewish festivals were governed by the cycles of the moon. The woman, being with child, cried out, travailing in birth and in pain to be delivered.

Though her pains were great, she at last brought forth a man-child. Our condition is not like hers in terms of travail and pain, but in bringing forth a man-child, we do share in her experience.

The Dragon's Threat. When the man-child was ready to be born, the dragon stood ready to *devour* it. In Scripture, Pharaoh, king of Egypt, is called the "dragon." Egypt is also a symbol of bondage, and in the spiritual sense, Rome is called "spiritual Egypt." The prince of this spiritual Egypt—Antichrist himself—and his followers seek to devour the man-child. The Antichristian party can rightly be compared to the Egyptians, for they seek to hold God's people in cruel bondage, just as the Israelites were oppressed in Egypt.

When Israel was delivered, Moses sang a song of praise (Revelation 15:3). So too, when the church is delivered from Antichristian bondage, the saints will sing the song of Moses, but with the addition of the song of the Lamb. These "Egyptians" would prefer the man-child to be destroyed, just as Pharaoh commanded that the male children of the Israelites be slain while allowing the females to live.

The Antichristian party would have been content with a mild and superficial reformation—a slight moderation of abuses. But when they saw the work of God rising higher, they became enraged. They longed to devour this work and prevent its birth. But despite their vexation and opposition, the man-child has been born and lives. God has, in part, taken away our reproach, just as Rachel exclaimed when she bore a son, "God hath taken away my reproach" (Genesis 30:23).

The Removal of Reproach. We once lay under reproach among the surrounding nations. People said, "England is returning to popery. Bishops rule there, and they drive out the godly ministers and the faithful people." But now, in large measure, this reproach has been taken away. The reproach of God's servants before our king and nobles, we trust, has also been wiped away.

In Hosea 7:3, it is written: "They make the king glad with their wickedness, and the princes with their lies." This was spoken of the ten tribes during their apostasy from the true worship of God. In those days, godly men could not conform to false worship and were forced to go to Jerusalem to worship rightly. There were courtiers who delighted in spreading lies about these faithful people, painting them as rebels and troublemakers to the king and the princes.

Similarly, in our time, some have sought to slander the faithful by inventing stories about them. Oh, how eager they have been to spread tales of "Puritan mischief" at court! No matter how outlandish the lie, it was enough if it served to make the king and nobles laugh and cast scorn upon the Puritans. They practiced the maxim *Fortiter calumniare, et aliquid haerbit*—"Slander boldly, and something will stick." But we trust that God has delivered our king and nobles from the influence of such men and has in some measure cleared His people from reproach before them. This is a mercy that we ought to take note of and give thanks for, as it is in line with God's promise in Revelation 12:10: "Now is come salvation, and strength, and the kingdom of our God, and the power of his Christ: for the accuser of our brethren is cast down."

The Greek term for "accuser" (κριτήγρας) refers to one who brings accusations before the king—unlike the Greek term παρακλήτης, which refers to one who intercedes on behalf of another. The accuser seeks to destroy, but the advocate seeks to defend.

The Man-Child Must Be Adorned. Now that this man-child has been born, let it not remain naked and bare. Let ornaments be placed upon it to beautify and glorify it, as described in Ezekiel 16. There, God depicts the birth of Israel as that of a helpless infant, covered in blood and abandoned. But God washed and adorned the child, placing jewels and ornaments upon it to make it beautiful.

What were we, not long ago, but a nation like a child left in its blood? But God has begun to cleanse us and calls upon you, right honorable leaders, to beautify this work of reformation that has begun. Your duty is to make it glorious—not merely in its beginnings but in its completion. This involves purifying the church, maintaining its true spiritual beauty, and ensuring that the entire kingdom shines as a testimony to all the reformed churches of the world.

Would it not honor God to end the reproach cast upon His people by offensive nicknames such as "Puritan" and "Faction"? If defamatory words against private citizens are deemed punishable, how much more should slanders against God's faithful servants be condemned?

Whatever wisdom suggests as necessary for adorning and furthering this work of reformation, pursue it with all your strength. By doing so, you place jewels, bracelets, and ornaments upon this man-child, making it beautiful in the sight of all who love Jerusalem.

A Sudden and Wonderful Mercy. Isaiah 66:8 asks: "Who hath heard such a thing? Who hath seen such things? Shall the earth be made to bring forth in one day? Shall a nation be born at once?" This verse speaks of the extraordinary and sudden nature of God's mercy. Our present mercy is like this—wonderful and sudden.

Cardinal Pole once cited this passage in a letter to Pope Julius III, marveling at how quickly popery had been re-established in England during Queen Mary's reign. He wickedly applied the text to that tragic event. But today, we are called to sanctify God's name by applying this scripture rightly—to praise Him for the sudden and extraordinary mercy He has shown us.

If any people in the world have reason to look upon God's work with amazement and exclaim with the prophet, "Who hath heard such a thing? Who hath seen such things?" it is us. This is the *work of the Lord*, and it is marvelous in our eyes.

God has dealt with us in an exceptional manner, beyond His usual dealings with nations. To experience such a reformation—so sudden, so significant, and yet accomplished peaceably—is astonishing. That such a great change has occurred with so little upheaval in men's hearts, and yet without conflict, is truly a miracle of our time.

A Cause for High Praise. Other mercies call for gratitude, but this calls for the highest praises of our God, to be in our hearts, on our lips, and shown in our lives. Future generations will scarcely believe the records of what God has done. If we recount even half of the events, they will think we are exaggerating. God's mercies are as high above our expectations as the heavens are above the earth.

The wonder of God's deliverance *should* fill us with awe and lead us to echo the song of Moses in Exodus 15:11: "Who is like unto thee, O Lord, among the gods? Who is like thee, glorious in holiness, fearful in praises, doing wonders?"

That ancient deliverance from Egypt was a type of the church's deliverance from Antichristian bondage. Therefore, we again take up the song of Moses and the Lamb, as recorded in Revelation 15:3-4: "Great and marvelous are thy works, Lord God Almighty; just and true are thy ways, thou King of saints."

What God has done for us is enough to silence atheism and strengthen our faith against all doubts. It is an enduring testimony of His power, His justice, and His covenantal faithfulness. Let us stand in awe, not only at the judgment we escaped but at the overwhelming and miraculous mercy that we have received. "Who is like unto thee, O Lord?" Surely, our hearts must overflow with gratitude and praise for the wonders He has performed.

We have long wondered what God intended to do with so many of His precious saints in England and with the countless prayers of His people—prayers both of those now in heaven and of those still living—which we knew He had stored up with Him. Now, God has revealed His purpose and done great things for us. We now see the mercy He had in store for His people. We now see a gracious answer to prayer. We, who once feared we would be the generation of God's wrath, have instead become the generation that inherits the plentiful harvest of our forefathers' prayers.

In what He has done for us, God has exceeded our faith, our hopes, our very thoughts—yes, even beyond our senses. When we *marvel* at His mercies, we find them beyond even our capacity for admiration. As it is written in Numbers 23:23: "Surely there is no enchantment against Jacob, neither is there any divination against Israel: according to this time it shall be said of Jacob and of Israel, What hath God wrought!" So now, we may say, and future generations after us will say: "What has God wrought!"

Our Response to God's Greatness. Let us, then, consider the great things God has done for us. And as 1 Samuel 12:24 exhorts, "Only fear the Lord, and serve him in truth with all your heart: for consider how great things he hath done for you." This applies to England today, in light of the mercies we have received. But oh, that it may also be said of us in regard to thankfulness and obedience: "Who has heard of such a reformation in the lives and ways of a people? Who has seen a nation turning to God as England has done?"

God has made us the recipients of extraordinary mercies. Should we not, then, become a wonder to the world in our obedience? Our service to God—our thankfulness—ought to be as extraordinary as the mercies we have received. Hezekiah is charged with failing to render due thankfulness to God, though he returned much. What, then, ought the leaders of this nation to do as a testimony of gratitude on behalf of the entire kingdom for the glorious things God has done for us? Surely, it must be something of great worth and excellence.

Mercy in Place of Deserved Judgment. Job 31:3 asks: "Is not destruction to the wicked? And a strange punishment to the workers of iniquity?" We have been workers of iniquity and yet have received *strange mercy*. It is as though God has made an exception from the general rule. Let us not blame ministers and others who, in the name of the Lord, have warned of dreadful judgments. According to the ordinary course of justice, their warnings were entirely appropriate. What if God, in His sovereign prerogative, has chosen to make us vessels of mercy instead? His Word of warning remains true and will forever stand.

Surely, God has a special love for England, as evidenced by His gracious and extraordinary dealings with us. Perhaps He remembers the "kindness of our youth," for England was the first nation in the world to receive the Gospel with the endorsement of supreme authority. As the historian Sabbellius records, *Prima provinciarum quae amplexa est fidem Christi*—"the first of the provinces which embraced the faith of Christ."

A Call to Encourage Our Hearts. Despite our many sins, I dare to say that God may receive more glory from England, and from our brethren in Scotland, than from the rest of the world. Surely, God has a good will toward England. He has done great things for us and will continue to do so. And you, Right Honorable leaders, He has raised up to be instruments of His glorious mercy toward us.

The Suddenness of God's Mercy. The prophet asks in Isaiah 66:8: "Shall the earth be made to bring forth in one day? Shall a nation be born at once?" These words highlight the suddenness of the mercy shown to us. If we had waited many years and received this blessing only at the end, we would have counted it worth the wait. But behold, the Lord has visited us suddenly and unexpectedly, as described in Isaiah 31:5: "As birds flying, so will the Lord of hosts defend Jerusalem." Just as birds fly swiftly to protect their young when danger arises, so has the Lord flown to our defense.

Instead of a flying roll full of curses (as in Zechariah 5:1-4), mercy has come flying *in upon us*. Isaiah 65:18 speaks of God's promise to "create Jerusalem a rejoicing, and her people a joy." The act of creation happens in an instant, and sudden mercies are the most joyful, just as sudden judgments are the most dreadful.

The Pace of God's Mercy. Consider the return of the Israelites from captivity. Their restoration was slow and full of interruptions. From the beginning of their return to the completion of the temple and the wall, seventy years passed. But for us, abundant mercy has come in just one year. And yet, some ungrateful hearts still cry out about the length of time it has taken. "Oh, how long has the Parliament sat, and yet things are not settled!"

Surely, if we could wait upon the Lord during times of judgment, we can now wait upon Him in times of mercy. We should wait patiently for the remainder of our blessings, seeing how much mercy has already come upon us suddenly and unexpectedly.

A Contrast from History. Cardinal Pole, in an address to Parliament during the reign of Queen Mary, marveled at how swiftly popery had spread again over the kingdom. He said: "It has come, not gradually like the strokes of a clock, but all at once, in a single moment." He used this to encourage the restoration of Catholicism.

But you, Right Honorable leaders, have an even greater encouragement in your work, drawn from the suddenness of God's mercy. God's hand has appeared gloriously for you and for us. There has scarcely ever been a more sudden transformation of a kingdom's circumstances since the world began.

What men accomplish suddenly often fails. Sudden conceptions prove abortive at birth, and hasty actions often produce misshapen and monstrous results. A wise man once said of those who rushed their affairs: "Stay a while, and you will finish sooner."

But the sudden work of God never miscarries. His sudden mercies are perfect, lacking nothing. What we have witnessed is a work of God's providence, carried out with wisdom and power. Therefore, let us not doubt or grow impatient. Instead, let us rejoice in His faithfulness and be confident that He who has begun this good work will bring it to completion. "Who is like unto thee, O Lord?" Surely, this day calls for our highest praise, for God has done what no human hand could do.

Let us bless His name forever, for His mercy endures from generation to generation.

The adversaries of God's work acted hastily, rushing forward without wisdom or patience. They believed they would devour everything in a single sweep, driving furiously like Jehu, son of Nimshi (2 Kings 9:20). They assumed that victory was assured and their work complete, but the Lord rebuked them.

The innovators who changed God's worship among the ten tribes were more cunning. Hosea 7:4 says: "They are all adulterers; they are like a heated oven, whose baker ceases to stir the fire, from the kneading of the dough until it is leavened." Though they were eager, they waited for their schemes to spread and leaven the hearts of the people before openly forcing their false worship upon them. But these men—the adversaries of our time—chose violence to thrust their innovations upon us. Had they followed the gradual approach, we would have been in grave danger of accepting their ways. But God turned their violence to our advantage.

We read how Mephibosheth's nurse, in her haste, dropped him, causing him to become lame (2 Samuel 4:4). Similarly, these men, in their reckless haste, crippled the very schemes they cherished. The projects they delighted in have become their ruin because of their impatience.

God's Sudden Works Are Strong and Sure. Though the sudden actions of men often lead to ruin, what God does suddenly is always strong and perfect. Created things—those directly formed by God—are made in an instant, yet they are perfect. The theological maxims stand true: *Creatisit in instanti*—creation happens in an instant, and *omne creatum perfectum*—all that is created by God is perfect. In contrast, things generated by creatures over time often turn out monstrous and flawed. Our sudden mercy is not flawed—it is glorious. This is why we must rejoice and praise the Lord.

God Will Bring to Completion What He Has Begun. Isaiah 66:9 declares: "Shall I bring to the birth, and not cause to bring forth? saith the Lord: shall I cause to bring forth, and shut the womb? saith thy God." This verse assures us that when God begins a work of mercy for His people, He intends to finish it. His loving-kindness is continuous (Psalm 36:10). It is a sign of human weakness to begin a building and fail to complete it. But when God lays a foundation, He will complete the structure. God does not raise a stage before the world, promising great things, only to leave it incomplete. When He opens a door, no man can shut it.

This was His promise to the church of Philadelphia in Revelation 3:7: "These things saith he that is holy, he that is true, he that hath the key of David, he that openeth, and no man shutteth; and shutteth, and no man openeth." Over thirty years ago, Mr. Brightman applied this promise to the church of Scotland. God opened a door to them, and none could shut it. Likewise,

God has opened a door to us, and no threats or schemes of men will succeed in closing it. God, who has brought us to the birth, will give us the strength to bring forth.

The Valley of Achor as a Door of Hope. God's promise in Hosea 2:15 is that He will give the valley of Achor as a door of hope. The word Achor means "trouble," named after the trouble brought upon Israel because of Achan's sin at their entrance into Canaan (Joshua 7). Many interpret this verse to mean that God will turn the troubles of His people into blessings, making them pathways to mercy—a sweet and comforting truth.

However, the Holy Spirit in this passage seems to allude to something deeper. The promise in Hosea 2 is part of God's assurance that He will restore apostate Israel and take her back as His spouse in loving communion, as seen from verse 14 to the end of the chapter. In Jewish marriages, it was customary for the bridegroom to give his bride a vineyard or a piece of land as a dowry, symbolizing his love and commitment. This dowry was an expression of his future kindness and a promise of further blessings to come.

Similarly, God, in *renewing His covenant* with His people, promises to give them the valley of Achor—not as a symbol of trouble, but as a fruitful and blessed inheritance. Isaiah 65:10 affirms this, stating that "Sharon shall be a fold of flocks, and the valley of Achor a place for the herds to lie down in, for my people that have sought me." This fruitful valley signifies God's abundant mercy—a down payment on the greater blessings He has in store.

Mercy as a Door to Greater Mercies. God's present mercies to His people are not the end but the beginning—the evidence and the pathway to greater mercies. When He begins a work of mercy, He will see it through to completion. When God brings His people to the point of birth, He will not leave them without the strength to deliver.

Therefore, we must take courage and rejoice. The adversaries thought they could devour the child before it was born, but the man-child has been brought forth by God's hand. The same God who has opened the door of mercy will continue to open doors of hope and blessing.

Our task is to *trust* Him, to praise Him for what He has done, and to expect with confidence the greater mercies yet to come. God does not merely start a good work—He carries it through to its glorious conclusion. Let us, then, "rejoice with Jerusalem, all you that love her; be glad with her and rejoice with joy." May we remember that the sudden mercies we have received are not only evidence of God's faithfulness but also promises of His ongoing and future grace.

When man begins a work, he cannot guarantee its completion. Often, the work falters and fails to reach its intended outcome. But when God begins a work, it will not falter. The adversaries of God's people devised their plans with evil intent, yet they could not bring them to fruition. Their schemes failed at the outset because God *was not in them*—blessed forever be His name for causing them to fail. But when God brings His work to the birth, as He has done in these great mercies, He will also provide the strength to bring it forth. Therefore, "Rejoice with Jerusalem, all you who love her, and be glad for her."

Let us not darken our joy this day with doubts or fears expressed in sentiments such as: "The work is not yet finished. What is done may still be undone. The child is not yet fully born; it may be stifled at the moment of delivery." Though some parts of the work remain in progress, and some hopes are yet to be fulfilled, do not let your hearts be troubled. The work that God has begun will certainly be brought to completion. God has begun something that He will not abandon until it reaches perfection.

God Will Strengthen His People Against Antichrist's Threats. Antichrist shall never prevail as he once did. God has poured out His Spirit upon His saints, and they will never again bow their backs in submission to false worship or tyranny. As the foundation of the temple was laid in Zechariah 4:7, the people cried out: "Grace, grace!" This is the cry of our hearts as well, for we know that it is by God's grace alone that the work is established.

It is true that when a man acts according to the strength of the flesh, he cannot boast while putting on his armor, for victory is uncertain until the battle is won (1 Kings 20:11). But when we rely upon God, we may rejoice at the beginning of His work as if it were already accomplished. This was the confidence of Jehoshaphat, who sent singers ahead of his army to praise the Lord before the battle began (2 Chronicles 20:21). David also declared in Psalm 108:7: "God hath spoken in his holiness; I will rejoice, I will divide Shechem, and mete out the valley of Succoth." He praised God in advance for victory, confident in the certainty of God's promises.

Has God Spoken for Us? Yes, He has! Ezekiel 39:29 says: "Neither will I hide my face any more from them: for I have poured out my spirit upon the house of Israel, saith the Lord God." Surely, the Spirit of the Lord has been poured out upon His servants in this land, perhaps more than in any other place in the world. Therefore, the Lord will not hide His face from us, and He who has brought us to the birth will give us the strength to bring forth.

A Call to Courage and Constancy. You, the Worthies of the Lord, must display a spirit of courage, zeal, and constancy in this great work to which God has called you. As you have begun nobly, continue to "ride on prosperously" (Psalm 45:4). This is the prayer of the saints for you: "Gird thy servants with strength, O Lord, and make their way perfect before them." Do not be discouraged by the insolence and boldness of the Popish party. Though both God and man are against them, they still lift up their heads in arrogance and promise themselves future victories.

Yet, this stubborn pride is part of God's curse upon them. No matter how severely God rebukes them, they refuse to repent. Revelation 9:20-21 states: "And the rest of the men which were not killed by these plagues yet repented not of the works of their hands, that they should not worship devils... neither repented they of their murders, nor of their sorceries." And Revelation 16:9-11 adds, "They repented not to give him glory... they blasphemed the God of heaven because of their pains and their sores, and repented not of their deeds." Even if God appeared visibly from heaven and unleashed His wrath upon them, they would rage rather than repent. God has not granted them repentance unto life; therefore, they persist in rebellion and insolence until they sink into ruin. Their confidence *blinds* them to their imminent destruction.

Do Not Fear Their Confederacies. Isaiah 8:12-13 warns against fearing the conspiracies of the wicked: "Say ye not, A confederacy, to all them to whom this people shall say, A confederacy; neither fear ye their fear, nor be afraid. Sanctify the Lord of hosts himself; and let him be your fear, and let him be your dread." The adversaries may confederate, plot, and speak great words of power, but we must not be troubled by their schemes. Instead, we must honor the Lord in our hearts and trust Him. He who has brought us to the birth will surely give us strength to bring forth.

The great design of Tobiah, Sanballat, and their company was to make Nehemiah and his workers afraid so that they would abandon their labor (Nehemiah 6:13). But Nehemiah and his people were not afraid, for they trusted in God. Likewise, we must not be discouraged by difficulties or threats. As the Lord was with Nehemiah, so He is with us. He will make every mountain a plain before us (Zechariah 4:7).

The Fear of Our Adversaries. Though our adversaries appear hardened and enraged, they are filled with fear in their hearts. There are still great tasks ahead, but God has already accomplished wonders as unlikely as those yet to come. Let us crown these works with constancy, for steadfastness adds beauty and glory to the work. As Psalm 90:17 says: "Let the beauty of the Lord our God be upon us: and establish thou the work of our hands upon us; yea, the work of our hands establish thou it."

When God establishes the work of our hands, His beauty rests upon us, and His name is glorified. Therefore, let us move forward with boldness and faith, knowing that the work God has begun will be perfected in His time. Let our joy be full, for He who has brought to the birth will not fail to bring forth.

This is a moment of divine significance, for this is God's appointed time to do great things for His church. There was a time when God raised up His servants to bear witness against the ways of Antichrist, not to bring immediate victory, but to uphold His truth and to strengthen their faith through suffering. In those times, God allowed Antichrist to prosper and ascend further, for the time of his downfall had not yet come. But now the appointed time has arrived. God is calling you to stand against him and his ways, for now is the day of vengeance and recompense for the blood that Antichrist has shed and for the evils he has wrought.

Those who now attempt to uphold him and his corruptions are like men born out of time. Had they come earlier, they might have succeeded in gratifying their ambitions for a season. But now they come at the most miserable disadvantage—they have entered the field of battle when *God Himself* is arrayed against them. Therefore, all of you who love Jerusalem, take heart and be courageous in resisting every Antichristian scheme in whatever ways God has called you. Your work will be glorious in His sight.

Persevere in Strength and Purpose. Natural actions are often strongest at their end. Let it be evident that the strength you have shown thus far comes from an inward principle of faith by growing even stronger as you continue. May none of you fall away or falter now. Remember the Lord's warning in Hebrews 10:38: "If any man draw back, my soul shall have no pleasure in him." You began this work with zeal and fervor—do not let that fire die down. You have made the adversaries tremble; let not your allies feel ashamed or disappointed in you.

The spirits of even the strongest saints can waver. Consider Elijah, who boldly confronted King Ahab, calling him the troubler of Israel (1 Kings 18:18). He summoned fire from heaven and prayed down rain. He slew 450 prophets of Baal. Yet when he heard of Jezebel's threat, he fled in fear (1 Kings 19:2-3).

Remain watchful and humble. Take heed, therefore, lest you become overconfident. *Watch and pray, that you may not fall into temptation* (Matthew 26:41). Let the weight of the great trust committed to you keep your hearts steadfast. Let your spirits rise above selfish desires—now is the time for true nobility of spirit. You may be weary from your long labors, as Gideon's 300 men were faint yet pursuing (Judges 8:4). Yet press on! You may feel that your strength is drained and your very bones are worn, but this weariness is your glory before both God and men.

Better is it to be spent in service to God than to waste your strength in sin or idleness. What is life for, if not to serve the Lord? You are like the olive branches in Zechariah 4:12, "emptying the golden oil out of themselves." You stand before the Lord, anointed for His service. Though your oil is precious, pour it out without regret, for the blessings of your sacrifice will return upon you and your descendants.

Embrace the Honor of Sacrifice. I have read of Pompey, who, when bringing corn to famine-stricken Rome through dangerous waters, declared: "It is necessary that corn be brought, not that I live." Your work, too, is necessary, even if it comes at great personal cost. You lose nothing, for the cause is worth your very lives. And in all your achievements, give glory to God alone. Let it be said, "Glory be to God on high, and peace on earth." If any of the honor clings to you, it will spoil the work. As Luther warned: *Feci, feci!*—"I have done this!"—is the cry that leads to corruption and turns glory into dregs.

Now is your time to fulfill the *vows* you made in private moments—perhaps on sickbeds—when you promised God that, if restored, you would serve Him wholeheartedly. God has granted you this opportunity to honor those vows. Use it well.

Shine as Lights in Your Communities. When you return to your homes and counties, carry the radiance of God's glory with you, as Moses did after spending forty days on the mount (Exodus 34:29). Appear before your people with wisdom, justice, zeal, and courage for God and His cause. The eyes of the nation are upon you. Since you represent God in your offices, it is fitting that you should reflect His character in your lives.

I have read of Scipio Africanus who, when offered a captive woman as a prize of war, refused, saying: "If I were a common soldier, I might indulge myself, but as a commander, I will not." In the same way, when you are tempted, remind yourselves: "If I were not entrusted with such a great charge, I might yield; but as one called to serve in God's cause, I must stand firm."

Guard the Honor of Your Calling. In 2 Samuel 1:21, David lamented that Saul's shield was "vilely cast away, as though it had not been anointed with oil." Let not your honor, as those anointed for service, be tarnished by sin. God has set you above your brethren, entrusting you with the welfare of the kingdom and the defense of His church. Do not let any sinful compromise dim the brightness of your calling. Keep your shields of faith lifted high, as proof that you bear the anointing of the Lord.

A Prayer of Blessing. If today God has placed in your hearts any resolve to act worthily for His cause and for His people, I echo the prayer of David in 1 Chronicles 29:18: "O Lord God of Abraham, Isaac, and Jacob, keep this forever in the imagination of the thoughts of the hearts of thy people, and prepare their hearts unto thee." May you be like the governors of Israel who offered themselves willingly for the service of the Lord (Judges 5:9). We will bless the Lord for you, and we will stir up all whom we can to join us in praising God for the great work He has done through you.

Let your hearts be steadfast, your hands strong, and your resolve unwavering, that the Lord may establish the work of your hands and crown it with His

Part 6: A Call to Rejoice

beauty and blessing. Isaiah 66:10, "Rejoice you with Jerusalem, and be glad with her, all you that love her, rejoice for joy with her, all you that mourn for her."

FINIS

Other Works at Puritan Publications by Burroughs

The Wonders of Jesus

Gospel Peace, or Four Useful Discourses

Gospel Worship, or, The Right manner of Sanctifying the name of God in General, in Hearing the word, Receiving the Lord's Supper, and Prayer

Jacob's Seed and David's Delight

Rules for Our Walking with God

Spots of the Godly and of the Wicked

The Excellency of Holy Courage in Evil Times

The Excellent name of God

The Saint's Inheritance and the worldling's Portion

The Excellency of the Soul

www.ingramcontent.com/pod-product-compliance
Lightning Source LLC
Chambersburg PA
CBHW031420160426
43196CB00008B/1002